Chief Pocatello

Photograph by A. J. Russell (1868–70) of "Snake Chiefs." The man in the center may well be Chief Pocatello since his facial features resemble those of Pocatello's brothers, Pokotel Pete and Pokotel Tom. The picture could have been taken on lower Bear River north of Corrine, Utah. *Photograph courtesy of The Oakland Museum.*

CHIEF POCATELLO
The "White Plume"

Brigham D. Madsen

Bonneville Books

University of Utah Press
Salt Lake City
1986

UNIVERSITY OF UTAH PRESS BONNEVILLE BOOKS SERIES

Copyright © 1986, University of Utah Press.
All rights reserved.
Printed in the United States of America.

Published with the assistance of the
IDAHO STATE HISTORICAL SOCIETY, BOISE, IDAHO.

Library of Congress Cataloging-in-Publication Data

Madsen, Brigham D.
  Chief Pocatello, the "White Plume".

  (Bonneville books)
  Bibliography: p.
  Includes index.
  1. Pocatello, Chief. 2. Shoshoni Indians—Biography.
3. Shoshoni Indians—History. I. Title.
E99.S4P636 1986   979.6'00497   86-6719
ISBN 0-87480-256-3

Cover Photograph: Pocatello Indians.
Utah State Historical Society

To

Ann, Phyllis, Mack, and Rod
*who grew up in the city named
for Chief Pocatello*

ALSO BY BRIGHAM D. MADSEN

The Bannock of Idaho (1958)

The Now Generation, editor (1971)

Letters of Long Ago, editor (1973)

The Lemhi: Sacajawea's People (1979)

The Northern Shoshoni (1980)

North to Montana: Jehus, Bullwhackers and Muleskinners on the Montana Trail, with Betty Madsen (1980)

Corinne: The Gentile Capital of Utah (1980)

A Forty-niner in Utah: Letters and Journal of John Hudson, 1848-1850, editor (1981)

Gold Rush Sojourners in Great Salt Lake City, 1849 and 1850 (1983)

B. H. Roberts: Studies of the Book of Mormon, editor (1985)

The Shoshoni Frontier and the Bear River Massacre (1985)

Contents

Photographs

Maps

Preface

Throughout a period of several years in research and writing about the Shoshoni and Bannock Indians of southern Idaho and northern Utah, I have kept a file on the life and career of Chief Pocatello of the Northwestern Shoshoni. It has been my hope that someday enough information might surface to provide the story of his life, and a recent survey of the material revealed more data than it was thought existed. So, I offer this short biography hoping it will be of general interest—particularly to the schoolchildren and teachers of Idaho—and in memory of my first teaching assignment as the principal of the Pingree School, located just across the Snake River from the Fort Hall Reservation, one of the areas where Pocatello once ruled over his Northwestern Shoshoni band.

The fact that the second largest city in Idaho carries the name of Chief Pocatello is the result of the geographic accident that placed the junction of Union Pacific rail lines to Montana and to Oregon at Pocatello Station near the crossing of the small creek still bearing his name. Pocatello Station was a stagecoach and wagon freighting stop on the Montana Trail as early as 1863 and thereafter functioned as a "swing" station for Ben Holladay's Overland Stage Company and, later, for Wells Fargo & Co.'s stagecoach lines. When the Utah and Northern Railroad reached the Fort Hall Reservation in 1878, it was convenient for the officials of the road to adopt Pocatello Station as the name of their new railroad junction.

The story of Chief Pocatello, or the "White Plume" as Col. Frederick W. Lander called him in 1858, deserves to be told even if his name had not become attached to an Idaho city. He was an Indian leader of consequence and had an important influence on some major events in the history of the Utah-Idaho area. An independent and audacious leader of a large band of Northwestern Shoshoni, Pocatello very early attracted the attention of Mormon settlers, government officials, and newspaper editors, some of the latter including scribes of the Sacramento and San Francisco journals. Finally forced to move to the Fort Hall Reservation, he never adapted well to the confinement of reservation life and remained the free spirit he had always been.

In the process of researching Pocatello's life over an extended period, the staffs of the following libraries and archives who helped locate materials have changed so many times that it will be best to express appreciation for their assistance in general terms: U.S. National Archives, the Federal Archives and Records Center in Seattle, Bancroft Library, Huntington Library, Idaho State Historical Society, Utah State Historical Society, Nevada State Historical Society, University of Utah Library, Utah State University Library, Brigham Young University Library, Idaho State University Archives, archives of the Church of Jesus Christ of Latter-day Saints (LDS), and the Fort Hall Indian Agency. I am particularly indebted to Brent W. Marley of Idaho State University, Charles S. Peterson of Utah State University, and Merle W. Wells of the Idaho State Historical Society, who read the entire manuscript and offered valuable suggestions for improvement. I, of course, accept responsibility for any errors which may have crept into the text and for the interpretation and judgments concerning Pocatello and his times.

Brigham D. Madsen
Salt Lake City, 1986

I was enabled first to obtain an interview with
ten warriors, an outlying party of the band of
Po-ca-ta-ro or the "White Plume."

Frederick W. Lander
Camp on West Branch of
Raft River, Fifteen miles from
City Rocks, August 16, 1859

Chief Pocatello

1
Prologue

In significant ways, Chief Pocatello's story begins with his mother. She was a member of a small Grouse Creek band of Northwestern Shoshoni whose homeland lay near City of Rocks on the present Utah-Idaho border, and the story of her capture and escape involving a Plains Indian war party has become a legend at the Fort Hall Reservation. It seems proper to introduce Pocatello by recounting his mother's courageous adventure. Dr. Minnie F. Howard of the city of Pocatello recorded the narrative on December 18, 1940, as related by Mrs. Jeannette Lewis, a granddaughter of Pocatello's mother. As Howard wrote, "One may understand his traits if the very tragic story of his mother is known."[1]

A raiding party of seven Assiniboin warriors on foot attacked a small group of Northwestern Shoshoni on the Raft River—among whom was Pocatello's mother, Widzhebu or "Cunning Eye"—in the spring of the year, sometime in the early nineteenth century. Widzhebu had her two-year-old daughter with her and was expecting another child in the fall. A young niece was captured with her, and the two women and the child were guarded by an older man while the other warriors hunted game as they neared the Bannock Range southwest of Fort Hall. The women lagged behind the rheumatic old man, looking for a chance to escape, and eventually the younger niece ran to a safe hiding place. But hindered as she was with her little child, Widzhebu remained a captive.

When the other men returned, in their anger at the escape of Widzhebu's niece, they awarded Widzhebu to one of the young warriors as a wife. The new husband then wrenched the two-year-old child from her mother's back, choked her to death, pulled the buckskin dress off the child's body, and threw it in her mother's face with the words, "Keep that instead of the child for a souvenir."

Continuing their journey, they finally reached a larger Assiniboin camp, where they displayed scalps taken in the raid, including that of a brother of Widzhebu. She was forced to watch a scalp dance in honor of the victorious warriors. To insure that his new Shoshoni wife would not escape, each night during the travel to the plains of Montana, the husband tied her to him by a buckskin rope attached to his legs.

When the war party reached their home country in northeastern Montana, Widzhebu discovered that her husband had another wife, the mother of a four-year-old daughter. Resigned to her new situation and relieved to find out that her new mate apparently intended to treat her kindly, she assumed the worst of such chores as gathering wood and preparing meals. She soon learned from another Shoshoni woman from the Raft River area, a captive of the Assiniboins for so long that she no longer thought of leaving, that her husband's first wife was jealous and intended to kill her. Widzhebu, therefore, began planning an escape. Each day as she went out from the camp with the first wife's daughter to gather firewood, while the child was searching for sticks, Widzhebu began excavating a hole under the riverbank. It could be reached only by swimming underwater, and little by little, she provisioned it with dried meat.

On a day when her husband was away hunting, Widzhebu went out from camp for the usual supply of wood, accompanied by the little girl. In a spirit of revenge for the loss of her own child, Widzhebu killed the girl by hitting her in the head with a hatchet and then secreted herself in the hole under the riverbank. Hiding for three days while search parties were all around her, she finally left her hiding place the third evening and, traveling only at night, headed for the Raft River. Her food soon gave out and, tired, weak, and pregnant, she despaired of survival. But Widzhebu came upon the burial site of an Assiniboin warrior and appropriated the knife, bow and arrows, some dried meat, and a piece of buffalo robe left by his grieving relatives for the deceased's safe journey into the next life. Saved by the cache and now approaching the mountains, she began traveling by day. One night a coyote attempting to eat the dried meat from her backpack startled her.

Finally reaching the Raft River, Widzhebu was taken in by an old couple who had stayed behind at the winter camp while the rest of the Northwestern Shoshoni band had gone off on a hunting expedition. They directed her to the main camp where she was met with great joy by her mother, father, and her husband, "who isn't married yet"—which meant her spouse had not given her up for lost and had not yet remarried.

In the story Howard recorded, Widzhebu soon gave birth to a male child who came to be known as Pocatello. No doubt this romantic ending to a tragic incident would add a certain mystic flavor to Pocatello's life, but the truth is a little less romantic. As Jeannette Lewis corrected, what really occurred was the birth of a daughter. Pocatello was not born until three or four years after his mother's kidnapping. As for the niece who escaped early in the adventure, she never returned to the tribe and nothing was ever learned of her fate.

But for Widzhebu, the perils of a 600-mile journey across the plains of Montana and over the Continental Divide did not keep her from her family and homeland on Grouse Creek. The courage, fortitude, and determination she displayed would doubtlessly be an example to a son who would lead her people and whose independence of spirit would gain the respect and fear of white newcomers.

2

Beginnings

I was enabled first to obtain an
interview with ten warriors, an
outlying party of the band of
Po-ca-ta-ro or the "White Plume."

Camp on West Branch of Raft River,
15 miles from City Rocks,
August 16th, 1859.
Col. Frederick W. Lander

Chief Pocatello's emergence from wilderness obscurity in 1859 to enough prominence to engage the brief attention of Abraham Lincoln in 1864 was a remarkable transformation. During these five years, his name came to be known to Mormon leaders, Indian agents, and army officers in the Salt Lake area and newspaper editors and readers on the Pacific Coast, mostly as a dangerous and intransigent chief of an outlaw band of Indians. This perception was no doubt a mystery to him when all he sought was to ensure food and safety for his people. In so doing, he felt compelled to stand up to white men who refused to treat him and his band with equality and humanity.

That Pocatello's homeland, stretching from the Raft River along the arc of the northern shores of Great Salt Lake to Bannock Creek and the Portneuf River, lay outside of Mormon settlement seemed to place him and his tribe apart from the other Northwestern Shoshoni. Even modern Indian descendants of these bands consider him and his people to have been separate and distinct because of his independence. As army officer Frederick Lander pointed out in 1859, Indian officials had never seen or talked to Pocatello—so far as they knew—even though there had been agents in the Utah area since 1850. But Pocatello certainly interacted with whites because of his location at the junction of the California Trail and the Salt Lake Road. Irresponsible and uncaring emigrants killed his people for no apparent reason, and he and his young men struck back, but only in revenge under the precept of an eye for an eye. When massacres occurred along the trails, it was very easy to blame a sovereign and free Indian chieftain whose home lay across the roads when it was just as likely that other Shoshoni or perhaps the warlike Bannock were involved.

With game disappearing under the guns of white men and the formerly bounteous grass seeds no longer available because of grazing by hungry cattle, Pocatello and the members of his band faced starvation and destitution. The only relief was to haunt Mormon settlements during the winter season and depend on the largesse of "Big-um" (Brigham Young) and his settlers to provide some sustenance. Various Indian agents did their best to coax more funds from a reluctant government to help feed the natives but often to no avail. The record seems clear that Pocatello responded to these new and deteriorating conditions with some moderation as he watched the women and little children of his band face starvation. His freelance and bold demands on the white interlopers in his country attracted attention and led traders, government and army officials, and Mormon settlers to consider him a perilous threat to the safety and security of travelers and farmers alike. The white settlers could later reminisce about the terrible and warlike Pocatello who refused the passive and subservient role most whites expected of Indians in the mid-nineteenth century.

Army officers were especially incensed that Pocatello would dare to stand up to them, seeming indifferent to military authority. Approaching Lt. Ebenezer Gay's command nonchalantly in August 1859, he was put in irons but did not seem to have learned his lesson after he was freed. He was careful to keep himself and his warriors out of harm's way after the Bear River engagement of January 29, 1863, as Gen. Patrick E. Connor tried to capture him, but scornfully and with spirit faced Connor when the general interrogated him about raids on Ben Holladay's stage stations. A strong army officer met an equally strong Indian leader and the honors were even. Of all of Pocatello's observers, probably Frederick Lander came closest to understanding the proud young chief and called him the "White Plume" in recognition of his supremacy over his followers. But even Indian Agent Jacob Forney noted how Pocatello dominated his people who "acknowledge no Chief superior" to him.

Lander's recognition of Pocatello as the "White Plume" arouses speculation as to the origin of the nickname. It is possible that the army officer, who seems to have been somewhat of a romantic, likened Pocatello to the French leader, Henry of Navarre. In the battle of Ivry, which was fought about fifty miles west of Paris in 1590, Henry of Navarre, as the headstrong and courageous leader of a Huguenot army, defeated the Catholic Holy League. Before leading his army into the engagement, he ordered, "My friends, keep your ranks in good order. If you lose your ensigns, the white plume that you see in my helmet will lead you always on the road to honor and glory." Henry won the battle and, later, in 1594, after he had converted to Catholicism, was crowned Henry IV, King of France. [1]

The English historian and poet, Thomas Babington Macaulay, in 1824, honored Henry of Navarre's victory at Ivry in a poem. In line 22, Macaulay wrote:

> The king is come to marshal us,
> in all his armor drest,
> And he has bound a snow-white plume
> upon his gallant crest.

Continuing with line 29 and following, the poet next has Henry proclaim:

> And if my standard bearer fall,
> as fall full well he may,
> For never saw I promise yet
> of such a bloody fray,
> Press where ye see my white plume shine,
> amidst the ranks of war,
> And be your oriflamme to-day
> the helmet of Navarre. [2]

Lander's obvious admiration for the young Chief Pocatello could have sparked the army officer's imaginative reference to him as a Native American Henry of Navarre.

As with other Indian leaders, Pocatello faced an almost impossible situation as travelers and settlers continued to encroach on his homeland and to destroy food supplies. He did his best to keep his young warriors in check but never allowed himself to be dominated by the strangers overrunning his land while attempting, with much frustration, to carve out a new life for his people. A possible treaty with the U.S. government seemed to offer the best hope that, finally, a negligent Great Father in Washington might offer a way out of a seemingly impossible dilemma. With this brief overview of Pocatello's career in mind, let us survey the conditions making his name feared in the settlements and along the western trails of the Great Basin and Snake River.

In portraying Pocatello's life, it is necessary to describe how his particular band, the Northwestern Shoshoni, fit into the mosaic of the great Shoshoni Nation which, in the 1800s, extended from South Pass in Wyoming west to the present Winnemucca, Nevada, area and to Fort Boise in Idaho, north to the Salmon River country, and south to Utah Lake and Death Valley. Occupying much of the Great Basin and the Snake River country, the Shoshoni people came to be known rather indiscriminately and derisively as "Diggers" in the western Utah and Nevada desert areas or as "Snakes" in the Forts Bridger, Hall, and Boise regions. Even when more sophisticated travelers and public officials knew them as Shoshoni, there was still little effort to distinguish among the various bands. Eventually, by the time of the reservation period of the 1870s, Indian agents identified the different groups and defined the boundaries of their home areas. Before examining in detail the homeland of the various Northwestern Shoshoni bands and particularly that occupied by Pocatello's people, it will, therefore, be useful to describe the other major Shoshoni groups.[3]

The Eastern Shoshoni, under their famous Chief Washakie, claimed as their country the Wind River Mountains where their present reservation is located but also spent much time farther south, near Fort Bridger. Numbering about two thousand in the 1850s, they were a mobile, horse-owning and buffalo-hunting people with a strong tribal organization and the Plains culture usually found among those tribes who pursued the bison for a living. Washakie maintained mostly peaceful relations with the Mormon settlers who began to encroach on his southern domain after 1847 and with the thousands of emigrants who traversed the Oregon Trail, the "Holy Road" as some Indians sardonically called it. Occasionally, Washakie would lead his people to brief summer encampments in Bear Lake Valley where they would meet with some of the Northwestern Shoshoni to trade horses, bargain for brides, and have a general Indian fair. Pocatello was not always congenial with Washakie, but they had a neighborly relationship, nevertheless.[4]

The Eastern Shoshoni found greater compatibility with their fellow tribesmen immediately to the west, the Fort Hall Shoshoni and Bannock who made their winter camps in the Snake River bottoms near Fort Hall. This Shoshoni group of perhaps one thousand people had lived harmoniously for years with some six hundred Bannock, a Northern Paiute tribe which had apparently migrated from the desert areas of southeastern Oregon to the more propitious and well-watered region found at the confluence of the Portneuf and Blackfoot streams with the Snake River. While keeping their own language and identity, the Bannock lived alongside the more docile Fort Hall Shoshoni, hunted the buffalo with them, went fishing for salmon below Salmon Falls on the Snake River, and made annual trips to the camas prairies of central Idaho. The two bands often joined with the Eastern Shoshoni in annual buffalo hunts on the Wyoming and Montana plains during which activities the Bannock chief, Tahgee, usually shared leadership responsibilities with Washakie. The Bannock made a name for themselves in western history as a warlike and athletic people who eventually became embroiled in the Bannock War of 1878 when some of their young men attacked white herders whose pigs were destroying the camas plants, a basic part of Bannock-Shoshoni diet. Both tribes finally settled upon the Fort Hall Reservation established in their homeland in 1867. Northwestern Chief Pocatello maintained an amicable relationship with the Fort Hall people who were his closest neighbors.[5]

Directly north of Fort Hall, another Shoshoni group, the Lemhi, numbering about eighteen hundred and famous in history as Sacajawea's tribe, wintered along the Lemhi River, a southern branch of the Salmon. Under their strong and well-known Chief Tendoy, a man of peace like Washakie, the Lemhi were also a horse people who hunted the buffalo in western Montana but depended for subsistence chiefly on the salmon that migrated in great numbers to the spawning grounds on the Lemhi and Salmon rivers. Tendoy's tribe usually visited the camas grounds each year, and here Chief Pocatello and his band may have come in contact with them, but the two tribes were not close neighbors. When the gold discoveries of the 1860s in central Idaho and western Montana brought white settlers into Lemhi territory, Tendoy's people suffered a period of starvation. Their tiny reservation on the Lemhi River offered little relief. Under strong pressure from the Indian Office in Washington, D.C., the Lemhi finally agreed to move to the Fort Hall Reservation in 1907 where their descendants live today.[6]

Farther west in the Snake River Valley were two other bands of Shoshoni. The Bruneau Shoshoni, about three hundred people who lived along the river of that name, were not a horse people and lived chiefly on salmon with a supplementary diet provided by camas and other roots plus small game. Most of them went to the Fort Hall Reservation in 1869. They did not figure prominently in Pocatello's history. The second group, the Boise Shoshoni of more than one thousand individuals during the fur trade era, gained horses rather early in the late eighteenth or early nineteenth centuries, as did the other Idaho and Wyoming bands. They engaged in buffalo hunting on the Snake River plains and in the areas of Wyoming and Montana. They traveled widely in search of subsistence but also counted salmon and camas as principal foods. Their numbers were greatly reduced after 1862 by expeditions of miners in the Boise Basin. Captain Jim, son of the early and famous Chief Peiem, led a major segment of the Boise Shoshoni in the 1860s. He was a prominent leader at the Fort Hall Reservation in the 1870s where about three hundred of the Boise people went in 1869. Pocatello and his group interacted with the Shoshoni from Boise River especially during buffalo hunting forays.[7]

Another Shoshoni-speaking tribe, the Gosiute, lived south and west of Great Salt Lake, occupying the sparse Tooele, Rush, and

Skull valleys and extending to the Deep Creek Mountains and the dry areas of eastern Nevada. By the time of concentrated white occupation, these nine hundred or so desert dwellers had gained the derogatory appellation of "Diggers," although before the new emigrants had appropriated the springs and waterholes and overgrazed the grass cover, the Gosiute had lived well. True, their diet of almost anything that moved or grew might not have tickled the palates of more discriminating whites, but food habits do not always indicate the relative degree of civilization. The Gosiute had very few horses at first but gained larger herds by the late 1850s. Chief Pocatello's people were neighbors to the north of Great Salt Lake, but the salt desert west of the lake formed a barrier to much neighborly exchange between the two Shoshoni tribes.[8]

Many scattered bands of Western Shoshoni occupied northern Nevada, extending as far west as present Winnemucca and Northern Paiute territory. The Ruby Mountains and the Humboldt River Valley offered shelter, horse pasturage, and access to fish and game. Pinyon nuts, roots, grass seeds, and berries provided further sustenance until cattle herds and interference with water supplies began decimating their food supply. The Western Shoshoni numbered about eight thousand by the 1870s, although disease and loss of subsistence supplies had already reduced their population. The bands in the northeastern corner of Nevada were next-door neighbors to Pocatello's people, and there was much visiting back and forth between the two groups.[9]

Finally, mention should be made of two lesser groups too far removed from Pocatello's territory to have much contact with him but who spoke Shoshoni and were part of this large nation. The Southern Shoshoni occupied Death Valley on the extreme southern edge of the Great Basin. To the north, in the mountains of central Idaho, an unmounted band of Mountain Shoshoni (otherwise indistinguishable from the Lemhi) later gained horses and were then known as Mountain Sheepeaters. Occasionally, they may have encountered Snake River Shoshoni near the camas meadows south of their mountain stronghold yet probably had little to do with Pocatello and his people.[10]

With this brief description of the major groups of the Shoshoni nation who resided around the perimeter of Northwestern Shoshoni country—in eastern Wyoming, the Great Basin, and the Snake River Valley—it is time to examine in greater detail the last contingent, the Northwestern group, who occupied the center of this vast area and whose members included Chief Pocatello's band. By the early 1860s, the Northwestern Shoshoni still numbered about 1,500 people divided into ten major bands. Their homelands extended from Bear Lake Valley on the east to the northwestern corner of Great Salt Lake and to Salt Lake Valley on the south. The eastern and northern shores of Great Salt Lake, the lower Bear River basin, and the valleys of the Wasatch Mountains east of the lake were favorite haunts. In Cache Valley in northern Utah, Chief Bear Hunter, as war chief and equal in power and authority with his eastern neighbor, Washakie, presided over a concentrated group of Northwestern Shoshoni who found a good living in the well-watered vale. Lesser chiefs in the valley were Sagwitch, Sanpitch, and Lehi. Little Soldier and a subchief, Ben Simon, led a band known as the Weber Utes who were also Northwestern Shoshoni and who lived along the lower Weber and Ogden rivers. With the exception of these tribal leaders and Pocatello, the other Northwestern band headmen have not made a dent in western history and would be lost except for their names attached to the Treaty of Box Elder. [11]

Having divided the Shoshoni nation into nine different groups according to geographic distribution and subsistence activities, it must be added that they can also be examined linguistically. Though they all spoke a single Shoshoni language, they can be divided into four dialect groups. After the eighteenth-century linguistic divergence of Comanche from the Northern and Eastern Shoshoni, there remained four dialects. These are the Comanche, Western Shoshoni, Southern Shoshoni, and the Northern-Eastern Shoshoni, the latter having a single dialect with the political subdivision of Washakie's Wind River people into a separate band unit, compared with a large array of Northern Shoshoni bands. [12]

The homelands of the Northwestern Shoshoni were concentrated along the rivers flowing into the eastern and northern sides of Great Salt Lake and on the Raft River and Grouse Creek northwest of the lake. Locating the various subsistence areas and villages of these bands as their camps existed at the time of white settler invasion in the 1850s requires, first of all, recognition that these small congregations of people moved about each year as food supplies dwindled or increased in the different areas. But the bands tended to place their winter camps in the same sheltered spots if sufficient subsistence were available. Anthropologist Julian Steward positioned Little Soldier's group at the confluence of the Ogden and Weber rivers; Bear Hunter's people on the Logan River in Cache Valley; and a series of three winter camps, probably under Sagwitch and Sanpitch, on the lower Bear River a few miles above its entry into the Great Salt Lake. Between Bear River and Blue Creek, near the north shore of the lake and west of present Corinne, there was a village of about twenty-three families with another camp located on upper Blue Creek. Fourteen families wintered at Kelton on the northern point of Great Salt Lake, and about six families found shelter at Lucin near the Utah-Idaho border. About twelve families were scattered along Grouse Creek, and a small cluster of six families wintered near Lynn and another eight at Yost with a larger camp stationed on Dove Creek. This concentration of Northwestern Shoshoni in the extreme northwest corner of Utah were Pocatello's people. A final camp was usually located either on the Portneuf River or on Bannock Creek, depending on the vagaries of food supply or social interaction. Thus, the Northwestern bands were scattered in winter camps from Logan and Ogden, Utah, west along the northern shores of Great Salt Lake to the Nevada border and north to Bannock Creek and the Portneuf River. It must be remembered that mounted bands had to move their camps more in winter than in summer in order to keep their horses on decent grazing ranges. They may not have traveled such great distances, but they could not settle down in a winter campsite for more than a few days. Early British trapping expeditions in the Snake River area had to move camp often for the same reason.[13]

Utah Indian Superintendent Jacob Forney, in his annual report for 1859, enumerated six bands of about twelve hundred Northwestern Shoshoni who occupied the northern valleys of Utah and the Raft River–Grouse Creek area. By 1863, Superintendent James Duane Doty estimated their numbers at fifteen hundred divided among the ten bands with whom he signed the Treaty of Box Elder.[14]

All of the Shoshoni of Utah, Idaho, and Wyoming spoke the same language and were known to each other by the staple foods forming the basis of their diets. The people of the eastern and Snake River areas were called Kutsundeka or "buffalo eaters" and constituted the aristocracy of the entire nation. Next to them in social status were such fortunate groups as the Padehiyadeka or "elk eaters" and the Lemhi Shoshoni who were Tukudeka or "mountain sheep eaters." Further down the scale came the Agaideka, "salmon eaters"; the Yahandeka, "groundhog eaters"; the Pengwideka, "fish eaters"; the Kamuduka, "rabbit eaters"; the Tubaduka, "pine-nut eaters"; and finally, the Hukandeka, "seed eaters," known derogatorily as "dust eaters." Of course, all of the tribes might eat any of the above foods at different times depending upon the availability of various game or vegetables. Pine nuts were found in the Grouse Creek area, while rabbits were hunted in the sagebrush regions north of Great Salt Lake. Grass seeds constituted a very important part of the diet of all Shoshoni, the seeds being beaten off into baskets by the Indian women using special implements. The destruction of grasses by the large cattle herds of the white settlers constitute one of the bitterest experiences that "civilization" brought to the natives of the Great Basin and the Snake River plains.[15] In a recent interview, Dr. Sven Liljeblad has provided more specific information about the food habits of Pocatello's people. Liljeblad's "primary informant" was Jeannette Pocatello, a daughter of Pocatello who was about four years old when her father died. She reported that "Pocatello's people were known to other Shoshoni as wild wheat eaters when they occupied lands around Bannock Creek and Promontory caves; that they were pinyon pine nut eaters around City of Rocks, where several detached groves far north of other pinyon stands were available; and that Fort Hall Shoshoni and Bannock bands referred to Pocatello's crew as pinyon pine nut eaters as distinguished from their [Fort Hall] economy as limber pine nut eaters."[16]

A description of Shoshoni homelands is not complete without delineating the emigrant trails crossing this land bringing white

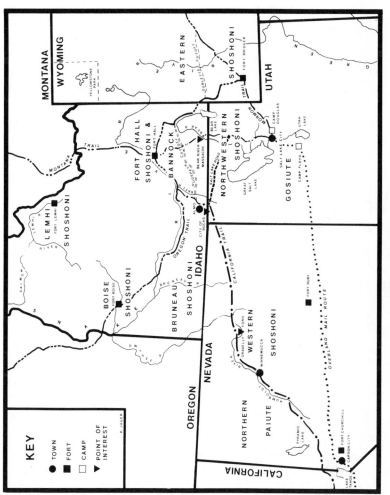

settlements into Pocatello's aboriginal territory. By the 1840s the
Oregon Trail was a rutted and well-traveled highway, emerging
from South Pass and traversing Washakie's Eastern Shoshoni country to enter Idaho near the Thomas Fork of the Bear River and on to
Soda Springs. From here it turned north and followed the Portneuf
River before crossing the Chesterfield Mountains to Ross Fork,
which it followed to Fort Hall. From the fort the road traveled along
the Snake River, past American Falls to the Raft River where the
California Trail branched off to the south. The road to California,
opened in 1843, went up the Raft River and Cassia Creek, then
through the jumbled grandeur known as City of Rocks and across
Granite Pass to Goose Creek and thence on toward present Wells,
Nevada. During the 1849 gold rush, B. M. Hudspeth and J. J.
Myers opened the Hudspeth Cutoff from Soda Springs through several ranges to rejoin the old road on Cassia Creek, near present
Malta, Idaho. Thereafter, most travelers used the cutoff rather than
the original trail. [17] Then, just thirty miles below the junction of the
Fort Hall Road with Hudspeth Cutoff, another trail, the Salt Lake
Road, was opened in August 1848 by Samuel J. Hensley. It coursed
from Salt Lake City north along the eastern shore of Great Salt Lake
and then across Bear River and west by north to a connection with
the California Trail in Junction Valley just north of the Utah-Idaho
border and a short distance south of City of Rocks. This road junction with its heavy emigrant travel was very close to the Northwestern Shoshoni villages on Grouse Creek. C. L. Craig, a member
of Indian Agent Garland Hurt's expedition of July 1855, speculated
that the trail junction was neutral ground between the various
Shoshoni and Bannock tribes, but Pocatello would have disputed
that conclusion. As Liljeblad puts it, Pocatello's "tough boys did
not tolerate other [Indian] people or let them into Raft river," which
was his central exclusive territory. All of the California Trail routes
(Fort Hall, Hudspeth, Salt Lake) and the Oregon routes traversed
Pocatello's country, which also encompassed their western
junctions. [18]

   The Salt Lake Road might not have come into existence without
the Mormon settlements in Utah. These settlements had an even
greater influence on Pocatello's Northwestern Shoshoni than did the

western migration. After establishing the initial colony at Salt Lake City in July 1847, Brigham Young began sending Mormon farmers north into the Ogden and Box Elder area along the eastern shore of Great Salt Lake until by the early 1850s substantial villages had arisen as far north as Brigham City, founded in the spring of 1851. This town was the nearest white community to travelers on Hudspeth Cutoff and the California Trail and, by way of the Salt Lake Road, was only about one hundred miles from the trails and the Grouse Creek Shoshoni camps. When attacks on wagon trains in the 1850s or 1860s began to take place near City of Rocks or in Marsh Creek Valley north of the Malad River, it was to the citizens of Brigham City that beleaguered emigrants looked for help. The various Northwestern Shoshoni bands also began to expect and receive food supplies from the Mormon farmers who were instructed by Brigham Young that it was better to feed the natives than to fight them. And, after all, white newcomers had taken over Indian lands and subsistence without any thought of compensation or much concern about how ploughing and seeding the land and large cattle herds were disrupting aboriginal life. [19] By the time of the national census of 1850, there were 11,380 people in Utah Territory, 8,000 of them in Salt Lake Valley. [20]

Although Mormon farms were beginning to encroach on Indian homelands in 1849, the Northwestern Shoshoni did not meet great numbers of whites until the gold rush of that year brought a constant stream of impatient travelers through native country. Emigrant travel up to that time had only amounted to an estimated 2,735 travelers to California. In 1849 alone, 25,000 gold seekers stormed the road to the diggings in California, 10,000 of that number through Salt Lake City and most by way of the Salt Lake Cutoff. The 1850 travel brought 44,000 more along the California Trail with 15,000 traveling via the Salt Lake Road. [21]

To the Shoshoni living north of the Great Salt Lake and in the Grouse Creek country, this horde of travelers brought a mixed blessing of grasslands denuded and food supplies curtailed but, at the same time, tremendous booty left along the road from overloaded wagons to crippled and worn-out cattle and horses, all of which the opportunistic Indians instantly appropriated. The rush to California

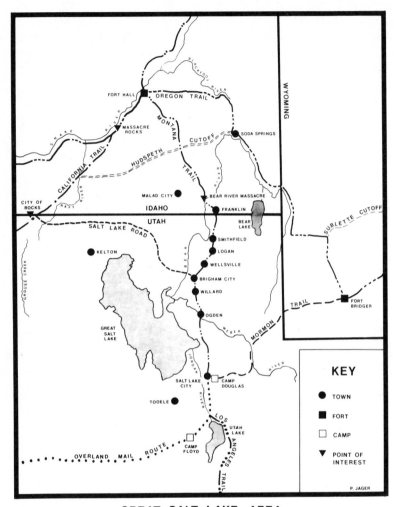

GREAT SALT LAKE AREA

not only changed the history of the American nation, but transformed Shoshoni life, especially for Pocatello's people who lived close to the California emigrant road. As the 1850s unfolded, Pocatello emerged as a consequential leader. Let us now look at his origins and examine the life he led prior to the gold rush.

3
From Grouse Creek to a Chieftainship

Whereas Pocatello's mother was known to be a member of the Grouse Creek group of Northwestern Shoshoni, his father's origins are not well defined. Pocatello's father was probably also from the Grouse Creek band, although another member of the clan, LaSalle Pocatello, when in his eighties told an interviewer at the Fort Hall Reservation in 1980 that his (LaSalle's) father's paternal grandfather had been a Flathead named Cornell. LaSalle added the cryptic note that "if the people knew that I was from Flathead, I would have been left out from the census role." It would be interesting to speculate that Chief Pocatello was descended from the Flathead tribe on his father's side, but it is reasonable to conclude that his sire was a Shoshoni from Grouse Creek.[1]

Pocatello was born in the Grouse Creek area probably sometime around 1815.[2] This approximate date is supported by U.S. Army explorer Frederick W. Lander's statement that after his meeting with Pocatello in the summer of 1859, he referred to the Indian leader as "this young chief." Also anthropologist Liljeblad has indicated that Pocatello had already become chief of his Grouse Creek village by the time of white immigration. Working within these two constraints, it may be reasonable to conclude that his birth about 1815 would place Pocatello in his early forties at the time of the Lander meeting. In 1884, Judge Taylor Oliver, who owned a ranch near Pocatello's home on Bannock Creek, estimated the chief to be seventy years of age.[3]

The name, Pocatello, has been given various meanings by imaginative whites over the years, but the origin remains obscure. The first written account came in an August 11, 1857, entry in the journal of Dimick B. Huntington, Mormon guide and Indian agent, who met the Shoshoni chief and called him "Koctallo."[4] Two years later, Lander interpreted it as "Pocataro."[5] Some writers have insisted that the name was given the Indian leader by whites and meant "he who does not go by the trail"[6] or "he does not keep to the road" because of his "style of ambush."[7] And proceeding on the theory that white men gave him the nickname of Pocatello, others have maintained that the name came from a town in Jasper County, South Carolina, Pocataligo, a Yamasee Indian village. The amateur linguists who applied this explanation may have been intrigued by the report of a contemporary who had viewed the Yamasee War of 1715 and reported that these warlike Indians were everywhere "killing all they meet . . . Lying Skulking in the Bushes and Swamps . . . [so that] we know not where to find them nor could follow them if we did so that we may as well goe to war with the Wolfs and Bears." At least a few angry whites of the 1850s through the 1870s would have considered that a good description of Pocatello's tactics.[8]

Indians, too, had different names for Pocatello. The Hukandeka Shoshoni of Grouse Creek called him Tonaioza, meaning "Buffalo Robe," when they did not refer to him as Kanah, a name he earned as the result of the gift of an army coat to him by Gen. Patrick E. Connor during the signing of the Treaty of Box Elder. Because there is no "l" sound in the Shoshoni language, the people of Fort Hall express the name of Pocatello as Pokendara, which is as close as they can come to pronouncing something foreign to them. Pocatello, according to Jeannette Pocatello Lewis, never used that name but called himself Tonaioza.[9] Perhaps Dimick B. Huntington should be given credit for inventing the word, Pocatello, or at least anglicizing what he heard when he asked the chief's name. As any reader of Huntington's journal will soon discover, he was a unique speller, "mutch" more interested in getting the facts down than in the exact reporting of an Indian's name.

The boy, Tonaioza, grew up during a "period of pleasant contact" with white fur traders who caused very little disruption in the Indian way of life and who introduced metal pots, steel knives and axes, firearms, and other accoutrements of civilization to the eager Shoshoni. [10] With the help of the new tools, the Grouse Creek people improved their subsistence and food-gathering activities. Various families would join forces where food was plentiful and then break up into self-sufficient family groups when scarcity faced them. Before the advent of horses in the 1840s, Tonaioza's father and mother would have been constantly on the move in search of food for themselves and their offspring.

When winter came perhaps as many as twenty or more families would find a sheltered spot to erect their tipis under the command of the village chief. Here, clay pots made from a special soil found along the Bruneau River were used for storage and cooking, and baskets the women wove held the seeds, roots, and salmon obtained during the gathering season. The men might be making arrow points from the obsidian they had secured from the Big Butte in the plains north of the Snake River, and the women would be occupied in fashioning rabbit-skin blankets once the cooking and wood gathering offered a respite.

In the starving period of early spring, the boy Tonaioza might suffer a few pangs of hunger along with his parents and brothers and sisters. But as soon as dry weather came and the snow was gone, there would be roots to dig and small game to hunt. By late May the family might join with others to travel below Shoshone Falls on the Snake River to harvest a supply of salmon to be dried for next winter's use. Along the way the children would aid their mother in gathering bird's eggs or large ants to be roasted on the coals. Before the salmon run, the more adventurous families would travel on to the camas prairies in south-central Idaho to gather a supply of the roots and engage in a week's general fair of barter, trade, and games with other Shoshoni and with the Nez Perce who, in later times, traded off their prized horses for buffalo robes from the eastern tribes. Tonaioza's father and mother would have pine nuts and seeds to exchange for buffalo skins and other desired articles. In the late summer and early fall, chokecherries and other berries were gathered and pounded and dried into small cakes. Among the staple foods of the Grouse Creek people were pinyon nuts which flourished in their territory. Gathering and roasting them occupied much time in the late fall. And always, Tonaioza's mother and the other women spent many hours beating seeds from the luxuriant grasses that covered the moist hillsides. With their baskets full, the women could then use the seeds for flour to bake into cakes or as a very nutritious mush.

The various families came together in the fall also to engage in communal antelope hunts near the Terrace Mountains and in Grouse Creek Valley. An antelope corral was built into which the animals were driven and then clubbed to death. After the first snow, the families held rabbit drives near Lucin. Several nets were used, each father of a family taking the responsibility for handling his own net. The men also did a great deal of hunting in the neighboring Grouse Creek and Goose Creek mountains for deer, mountain sheep, bear, fox, beaver, wildcat, porcupine, waterfowl, and such smaller game as pack rats. A few trout could be taken in Grouse Creek. And until 1840, buffalo ranged the Snake River plains in the Portneuf and Blackfoot river areas near Fort Hall, but, before acquiring the horse, the Grouse Creek people had no means of hunting bison.

The introduction of the horse in Pocatello's early years transformed Northwestern Shoshoni culture at Grouse Creek and in the areas north of Great Salt Lake. They began to range far beyond their old habitats, to wear the skin clothing of the plains, to dwell in skin tipis, and to choose bold and able leaders who could deal with the uncertainties of hunting the buffalo in enemy territory and meet the threat of white men encroaching on Indian homelands. No longer confined to Grouse Creek, Tonaioza and his family were at home in the areas north of Great Salt Lake, in Bear Lake Valley, and along Bannock Creek and the Portneuf River above Fort Hall. The meadows along the Raft River provided good pasturage for the new horse herds, and the even better grasslands of Portneuf River near the present city of Pocatello offered winter forage.

By 1840, the Grouse Creek people were a highly mobile band who continued the age-old pursuit of foods as before, but now could think of joining the Fort Hall Shoshoni and Bannock and Washakie's people in annual buffalo forays on the Wyoming plains. Also, their ancient home at the junction of the California Trail and the

Salt Lake Road would soon become a western crossroads for thousands of gold seekers and emigrants. The "golden age" of the fur trade was at an end, and new leadership was needed to cope with the problems that mobility and foreign intrusion were introducing.[11]

Before describing Pocatello's rise to power, it is necessary to examine the Shoshoni concept of leadership or chieftainship. As Merle Wells has expressed it from the work of Sven Liljeblad:

> Each band or unorganized extended family group had a few trusted leaders who gained their position through their success in persuading others to come along with them to hunt buffalo, dig camas, gather pine nuts, or go salmon fishing. . . . Each band had several trusted leaders who insisted upon explaining that they had about equal authority. They consistently rejected any system of authoritarian chiefs, and had chiefs only when Anglos insisted upon imposing that system upon them. Anglos had to appoint their Shoshoni chiefs in order to obtain them at all. . . . [Chief] was an alien concept that Pocatello would have been more than uncomfortable with.

Although most prominent Shoshoni band leaders considered themselves equal in rank, it must be said that as far as Pocatello was concerned he was more equal than the other headmen in his particular band. This perception of him as an outstanding leader was true not only of whites such as Frederick Lander but also in the eyes of Pocatello's own people. His authority over them, of course, varied from time to time but remained powerful throughout his career until his last years on the Fort Hall Reservation when he declined to exercise leadership as the Indian agents there wished. With this explanation made, we shall continue to call him Chief Pocatello in lieu of any better designation as the new leader of his people.[12]

Tonaioza, soon to be known as Pocatello, in about 1847 became the headman of Kuiya, a village of fifteen Tubaduka families located near present Lynn and Yost in Raft River Valley. Although young at the time, he demonstrated the personality, ambition, and independence of mind necessary to become the spokesman and leader of his people. Within five or six more years, he had extended his influence over another village, Biagamugep (near the later railroad freight sta-

As Indian Superintendent, Brigham Young sought to placate the natives with his feed-rather-than-fight policies, but there was constant friction nevertheless. *Utah State Historical Society.*

tion at Kelton north of Great Salt Lake), where the Kamuduka accepted him as chief. By the time of his first appearance in written history in 1857, he was also in control of other Kamuduka at Bannock Creek and at the bend of the Portneuf River and north to the present city of Pocatello. Perhaps as many as four hundred people acknowledged him as the head of these combined Northwestern

Shoshoni groups. It was a remarkable rise to power by one so young and testified to his leadership qualities and his willingness to challenge the Mormon settlers and the emigrant trains who were coming into his country. [13]

With Brigham Young's settlements pushing north from Salt Lake City as far as Brigham City by 1851, the long-time Indian residents of the land between the Wasatch Mountains and Great Salt Lake became impatient and angry as horse pastures and ancient camping sites were converted into plowed fields. Although Young, as superintendent of Indian affairs for newly formed Utah Territory, sought to placate the natives with his feed-rather-than-fight policies, there was constant friction nevertheless.

In the spring of 1850, a band of sixty-five warriors of Little Soldier's Weber Ute band, having suffered severe losses from a measles epidemic, left their winter camp near the mouth of the Weber River as did another Northwestern Shoshoni group under Chief Terrikee. Little Soldier kept his people away from the Mormon settlement at Ogden, but Terrikee's band returned in mid-August and began acting "very bad. . . . [They] would ride through grain fields and melon patches." [14] Fearing trouble, Terrikee sent his people away but was killed himself by a Mormon farmer, Urban Stewart, who mistakenly thought the chief was trying to steal corn. In retaliation, Terrikee's people killed one of the settlers. The remaining white families crowded into a fort and were only relieved when 150 militia troops hurried north from Salt Lake City to disperse the Shoshoni. [15] General Daniel Wells of the Mormon troops was so concerned for the safety of emigrants on the California Trail in the vicinity of City of Rocks and near Pocatello's homeland that he sent out five troopers to read a proclamation to the travelers:

> To the Emigration on the Road
> We have sent Master L. Robinson with a small detachment to inform you that a little difficulty having occurred with the Shoshones or Snake Indians, you should be on your guard, you should travel in companies and keep a good watch especially at nights. We do not know as there is any danger but "caution is the parent of safety" therefore be wise and harken to the counsels of wisdom.
>   Yours Respectfully,
>   By orders of Brigham Young
>   Gov. [16]

Wells dispatched another party of twenty-five soldiers to "get a talk" with the "Panaks and Shoshones" in the Fort Hall area.[17] Chief Pocatello may have been involved in this council along with other Indian leaders of the area. The Terrikee incident at Ogden certainly heightened tension between Mormon settlers and the outlying Northwestern Shoshoni to the north of Great Salt Lake.

As the 1850s progressed, other Mormon-Shoshoni differences surfaced, highlighting Indian displeasure and focusing attention on Pocatello who seemed always to be hovering on the outskirts of the northern Mormon settlements, posing a threat to plowing and planting. On July 3, 1851, a raiding party of Shoshoni drove off seven horses from Weber County. A company of fifty men sent in pursuit failed to recover the animals but did explore "Cash" valley which they pronounced "the best they had seen in the Territory for soil, timber and water," a discovery that helped advertise the valley and led to its eventual Mormon colonization.[18] When in 1852 Indian Agent Jacob Holeman began to complain to his superiors in Washington, D.C., about how the Utah Saints were taking over Shoshoni lands without compensating the dispossessed natives, his boss, Superintendent of Indian Affairs Brigham Young, indignantly replied that not only were the Indians not opposing the spread of Mormon farms but "have at various times solicited settlements to be made in their respective lands in order that they might be benefited in the articles of clothing and provisions. . . . Are not the Indians better fed, better clothed, and more peaceably disposed towards the whites than before their settlement among them?" Pocatello and the other Shoshoni headmen certainly looked to the Mormons for subsistence during starving times as the only alternative now that aboriginal homelands had been taken over and food supplies destroyed. Young concluded his argument with the observation that the Northwestern Shoshoni needed to be chastized on occasion when such discipline was usually "richly deserved."[19]

Despite their differences, Holeman and Young agreed in their suspicions that the Shoshoni of the Box Elder settlements were involved in raids on emigrant parties along the California Trail. An investigation proved that these Indians had a sizeable amount of American gold pieces which they claimed had come from trading horses with the emigrants. To reassure himself, Holeman made a trip to the California Trail at the Goose Creek Mountains in the early fall of 1852, but the Indians there told him they were only on a hunting expedition and were in no way disturbing the emigrants.[20] Pocatello's people were undoubtedly among those Holeman questioned. This was their home territory, and the incident illustrated why white officials and Mormon settlers alike soon considered Pocatello a major source of trouble for emigrant parties en route to California.

But western travelers were not the only whites threatened by the Northwestern bands, as David Moore reported in 1853. At Willow Creek in the Box Elder district, a mounted band of 150 Shoshoni raced into the settlers' camp at "full speed, whooping & yelling & singing their war song." The Indians defiantly turned their horses into the fields of corn, grain, and potatoes while helping to harvest the crops themselves. Moore described the Shoshoni as being "very bold and saucy."[21] The next day the natives challenged the settlers to come out and fight, having been excited by an Indian woman who was living with one of the white families and who told her people that the "Ammericans were going to kill them." After a council meeting, the warriors departed peacefully, but Moore reported, "The Shoshones are very bitter against us & say that this is their ground & they intend to have it. I cannot see how we can avoid a fight with them much longer."[22]

The hostile and threatening attitude of the dispossessed Shoshoni toward the Mormon settlers carried over to travelers on the California Trail, as observers tended to blame Pocatello for most of the attacks on emigrants. "Uncle Nick" Wilson, a white who spent part of his youth as an adopted member of Washakie's tribe, was especially vehement toward Pocatello. Because Wilson's memoir was written years after the events of his boyhood, one must be very careful in accepting his stories, but his recollection does describe graphically how the legend developed that Chief Pocatello was the most ferocious outlaw ever to haunt western trails. Wilson remembered a meeting with Pocatello and his band in 1854.

The Eastern Shoshoni under Washakie joined other tribes, including Pocatello's band, in a general fair in the Deer Lodge Valley of Montana about August of that year. Wilson's adopted mother warned him that Pocatello's Indians "were very bad and that they would steal me and take me away off and sell me to Indians that would eat me up." Wilson watched Pocatello's warriors conduct a scalp dance around six scalps taken from emigrants, one scalp being that of a woman with red hair and another that of a girl with dark hair. As the encampment was breaking up, Wilson went off to look for his horse, which had strayed away from the herd. He soon discovered that his Indian mother's fears were justified when one of Pocatello's band picked him up and carried him off on horseback. Seizing an opportunity, the white boy jumped off the horse but was lassoed by the warrior who began to beat Wilson with a quirt and then attempted to shoot an arrow into him. At this critical juncture, a party of Washakie's warriors appeared in the distance and after frightening off the would-be captor escorted Wilson safely back to his mother's tipi. Chief Washakie then lectured him for going off alone from camp while Pocatello and his band were around as they intended to steal him if they could to sell "for a great many ponies." The whole story may or may not be true, but it does indicate the fearsome reputation Pocatello had with many whites.

Wilson concluded his narrative by describing Pocatello as not being as large as Washakie and that the two chiefs were "never very friendly . . . [because] Pocatello wanted to kill and rob every white man that came his way," whereas Washakie wished to pursue a friendlier course. In fact, according to Wilson, "Pocatello called him [Washakie] a squaw, and said he was afraid to fight." Wilson appraised Pocatello (who, he claimed, had a Bannock wife and three children at the time) as "a sneaking and wicked looking Indian, . . . [whose] tribe did more damage to the emigrants than any other tribe in the west." The entire incident reads as though it was taken from one of the dime novels of the time but does describe the widely held notion that Chief Pocatello was a particularly dangerous and evil character.[23]

To return to more reliable sources, Brigham Young, in that same year of 1854, recorded in his Manuscript History that, in September, he had visited a large number of Shoshoni who had sent a deputation of chiefs asking for a meeting with him. There were seven chiefs with their bands assembled in a camp five miles north of Ogden. One of these Indian leaders could very well have been Pocatello who, by this time, was a leading figure among the Shoshoni of northern Utah. After a talk, Young distributed a few presents "but through lack of means not so many as desired." The chiefs departed with a feeling of friendliness and a desire to remain at peace with the white people.[24]

Amicable relations between Mormon settlers and the Northwestern Shoshoni continued throughout the next year, 1855, although one Salt Lake visitor to Box Elder did report that some Shoshoni from the Fort Hall area "under the pretense of gleaning, are committing great depredations on the wheat still in the fields."[25] To try to satisfy the needs of the Indians, Brigham Young granted I. and J. M. Hockaday permission to establish a trading post twenty-five miles north of Brigham City, in Pocatello's country.[26] Dr. Garland Hurt, Indian agent for Utah under Superintendent Young, discovered that not all of the Northwestern Shoshoni were satisfied with gleaning and new traders when he met a "rough looking set of fellows" east of the Deep Creek Mountains on the Salt Lake Road who had several head of American horses with their ears freshly cut and obviously stolen from emigrants. Hurt "lectured them severely" about such thefts. These warriors were in Pocatello territory and could have been members of his band.[27]

The frustration and anger of Shoshoni leaders in Utah and Idaho reached Agent Hurt in September 1855 when a number of "Snake Indians" and "northern Snakes," with perhaps Pocatello among them, met him and a group of Utes at Salt Lake City. The Shoshoni had come to the City of the Saints after hearing rumors that government officials wished to sign a treaty with them. In the grand council that followed, the Shoshoni complained "that they had permitted the white people to make roads through all their lands and travel upon them in safety, use the grass and drink the water, and had never received anything for it, all though the tribes around them had been getting presents." Hurt agreed that the Shoshoni cause was just. He reminded the commissioner of Indian affairs that the government had treated with other tribes for compensation for their lands and that, in addition, there was injustice to the pioneer settlers of Utah who were being "forced to pay a constant tribute to these worthless creatures, because they claim that the land, the wood, the water, and the grass are theirs, and we have not paid them for these things." Hurt asked for an appropriation so he could negotiate treaties with the Utah tribes.[28] He could have reinforced his views by reporting that during the summer Mormon herders had opened up the settlement of Cache Valley by driving 2,400 head of "Church" cattle into the valley and that the first settlers were already on the ground with new log homes.[29]

Occasionally, in a special gesture of Brigham Young's easier-to-feed-than-to-fight policy, a neighboring group of Shoshoni might be invited to join in a festive Pioneer Day banquet, such as that held on July 24, 1856, at North Willow Creek in the Box Elder area where fifty of the Indians and numerous citizens "partook of the bounties placed before them, much to their satisfaction and delight.[30] But such feasts only sharpened native appetites for more food requests to the struggling settlers.

After a decade of watching Mormon ploughs turn the soil of the Ogden, Box Elder, and the Cache Valley regions, the restive Northwestern Shoshoni encountered a new situation along with their Mormon neighbors when the Great Father in Washington, James Buchanan, decided to send an army to Utah to enforce federal law and bring Brigham Young's Saints to heel. This event also brought Chief Pocatello into public notice and presented him as a malcontent whose refusal to pay heed to government civil and military officials would make a place for him in western history.

For multiple reasons, which included the abhorrence of most Americans for polygamy but, more important, charges that the Mormon hierarchy was in despotic control of Utah Territory and was instigating Indian attacks, President Buchanan believed that a state of rebellion existed and that Brigham Young had to be replaced as governor. The Utah people learned on July 24, 1857, that an army of the United States was then on its way to depose Young as governor and superintendent of Indian affairs and install Alfred Cumming of Georgia as the new executive with a separate official in charge of Indian affairs.

During the next several months, Mormon guerrilla attacks on army supply trains forced the government troops into winter quarters at Camp Scott near Fort Bridger and negotiations finally achieved a settlement by a special commission. Gen. Albert Sidney Johnston's 2,500 troops thereupon made a peaceful demonstration march through abandoned Salt Lake City on June 26, 1858, and established their headquarters at Camp Floyd forty miles southwest of the city in Cedar Valley. For Pocatello and other Indian leaders, the Utah War was significant because it gave the impression that, first, if the government could attack the Mormons, it might be permissible for Indian tribes also to take liberties with the Saints and, second, that the event brought into the territory a large body of troops to be stationed permanently near the Utah capital. As Pocatello and other Shoshoni leaders soon learned, this could lead to dramatic and dangerous threats to Indian freedom and mobility.[31]

The arrival of Johnston's army caused much excitement and uncertainty among the Shoshoni of Utah and the Fort Hall area and resulted in efforts by Brigham Young and his various agents to quiet the Indians. The superintendent sent Dimick B. Huntington to East Weber on August 10, 1857, to visit Chief Little Soldier and found him and his people to be "Mutch Excited" because of a rumor that "Brigham was going to cut all the men's throats & take their women to wife." Huntington reassured Little Soldier and advised him "to be Baptised & then he could tell when the Gentiles told him a lie." The chief answered that "Tom had been Baptised & he lied all the time." The Mormon agent then explained that Brigham Young had warned the tribe that game was becoming scarce, that a famine was coming, and that the Indians should settle down and learn to farm "but they set down on their buts & Howled like so many Wolvs" instead of following Young's advice.[32]

The next day, Huntington went on to the "City of Brigham" to visit a large Shoshoni camp and found "Koctallo Pibigand Petort-Neet & their Different Bands 400 in number men women & children." He found them much excited also and afraid of being poi-

soned. After distributing six beef cattle and three wagonloads of
bread, potatoes, corn, and other vegetables as presents, he gave
them Young's instructions to lay in a supply of food for the coming
famine. Then, addressing Pocatello, as Huntington later reported:

> I had under stood that some of the tribe had stolen some of the Calafor-
> nians horses & mules   the Chief looked much down and after a little he
> said he had heard a little that they had & asked me if I was mad   I told
> him no then asked if Brigham was mad   I told him he could then tell
> me all about it & even show me whare the Horses was cashed in the
> mountains & left them feeling quite well.

In this very first written account of Pocatello, as many other white
officials were to do later, Huntington accused the chief and his
people of being implicated in attacks on emigrants on the California
and Salt Lake roads. And here, as often in future incidents, Pocatello
disclaimed any responsibility but acknowledged that some of his
young warriors might have been implicated, acting on their own
impulse.[33]

Returning to Ogden on the following day, Huntington found
some Mormons who wanted an Indian guide, so he returned to
Ogden's Hole to ask Pocatello's help in obtaining one. The chief
said that he had no one there who could serve but sent one of his
men to Brigham City to obtain the required guide. Huntington
then repaid the Shoshoni leader by making a "feast for 100 or more
Indians thare. The Breathren done first rate by the Indians."[34] Brigham Young continued his policy of feeding the various tribes and
trying to placate them.

On September 30, 1857, Young sent Huntington to visit another large encampment of Shoshoni of 120 lodges of a thousand
people at Farmington. The agent gave the Indians four wagonloads
of corn and melons while Mormon Bishop Chauncey West of Ogden
contributed four beef cattle. Then, Huntington attempted to enlist
the aid of the Shoshoni in rounding up any stock on the roads north
and west of Great Salt Lake to help deny the U.S. Army food
supplies:

> I told them that the Lord had come out of his Hiding place & they had
> to commence their work   I gave them all the Beef Cattle & horses that
> was on the Road to Cal Afornia the North Rout that·they must put

them into the Mountains & not kill any thing so Long as they can help
it but when they do Kill take the old ones & not kill the Cows or
young ones they sayed it was some thing new they wanted to Council
& think of it.[35]

Pocatello's people were very likely part of this large assemblage who
received Huntington's radical proposal.

In one of his last reports as superintendent of Indian affairs for
Utah, Brigham Young described the situation as of September 12,
1857.[36] He complained that the Indian Office had failed to make
the necessary appropriations so that he could help feed the Indians,
who were a "sore tax upon the people." In addition and partly because of the lack of expense money, Young reported of Pocatello's
band, "West and along the line of the California and Oregon travel,
they continue to make their contributions, and I am sorry to add
with considerable loss of life to the travellers. . . . I find it the most
difficult of any portion to control." He explained further that emigrant lives and property were being lost in this area because a party
of about four hundred "returning Californians" had, during the last
spring, shot at every Indian they could see, shooting "them down
like wolves." He explained that Mormon farmers were in the habit
of giving Indians met on the road presents of food and tobacco and
that the natives approached emigrants with the same expectation
only to be shot down.

Superintendent Young was certain the coming of the troops
made it difficult for him to restrain the Indians of Utah: "The sound
of war quickens the blood and nerves of an Indian." He repeated that
the worst attacks on emigrant parties were perpetrated by a "few
called 'Snake diggers' who inhabit as before stated along the line of
travel west of the settlements." Chief Pocatello and his band were
beginning to earn their unfavorable place in western history. Young
continued that when news came of the approach of Johnston's army
some of the Shoshoni had attacked herds of Mormon cattle because
"they seemed to think if it was to be war they might as well commence and begin to lay in a supply of food when they had a chance."
The superintendent concluded his report with three recommendations: (1) that travelers discontinue the practice of shooting down
every Indian they happened to see, (2) that the government should

give him a more liberal appropriation for Indian supplies, and (3) that the troops must be kept away because their presence only added to Indian hostility. A year later, on May 3, 1858, Dimick Hunting-ton supported Young's last contention by reporting that a group of Utes told him "the soldiers was bad they gave them nothing to eat & all they did was to use their squaws & had made them all [angry]."[37] Most of the tribes feared the troops and stayed as far away from them as possible.[38]

By the end of Brigham Young's tour of duty as superintendent of Indian affairs in 1857, Chief Pocatello had come into prominence as the aggressive and dangerous leader of the Northwestern Shoshoni band who controlled the California and Salt Lake trails north and west of the Great Salt Lake. His origins at Grouse Creek with an unknown father but a mother whose early history bespoke a woman of energy, determination, and courage, introduced Pocatello to harsh conditions and a cultural environment conducive to either subjugation or resolute leadership. That he rose to a chieftainship over a band of about four hundred Shoshoni at a very young age underscored his qualities of ambition, independence, restless en-ergy, and fortitude. The Utah War and the arrival of Johnston's army introduced a new element into the lives of Pocatello and his people, an event which was to bring greater notoriety to the North-western Shoshoni leader.

4

Mormon Settlers and Army Troops

As Gen. Albert Sidney Johnston's troops settled in at Camp Floyd, Utah's current Indian agent, Jacob Forney, made his first trip to the Humboldt River area "to visit the Indians, on the great Northern Rout to Calif." This was late in September 1858. At the first crossing of the Raft River, east of Goose Creek Valley, two men from Pocatello's band presented Forney with a letter from Col. Frederick W. Lander, superintendent of the Honey Lake Route, dated City of Rocks, September 15, in which Lander assured the Indian agent that "these Indians are friendly. Po-ko-telle, their chief, also exhibited other testimony to prove his friendship towards white men. The only thing calculated to excite suspicion is that this chief claimed independence of the tribe to which his band properly belongs. This is however, a common failing with ambitious young Sub-Chiefs, especially when the band is large. This Band has evidently never been seen & talked to, by any Indian official."[1] There was, thus, evidence from the beginning that the young Pocatello's independence meant that he and his followers were to be considered on their own merits and would not be lumped together with all other Shoshoni in the Great Basin or on the Snake River. In fact, all Shoshoni groups were independent and did not get along well with other bands.

Agent Forney later emphasized that Pocatello's band was indeed to be considered separate from the other Northwestern Shoshoni by writing to the commissioner of Indian affairs on September 29, 1859, that while there were about one thousand Shoshoni who ranged "through Salt Lake, Weber, Ogden, Bear River, Cache and Malad valleys . . . one band, of one hundred and fifty to one hundred and eighty, mostly confine themselves to the regions along the northern California road, from Bear and Malad rivers to the Goose Creek mountains."[2]

The day following his initial meeting with Pocatello, Forney met with all members of the band, and he reported of the meeting:

> This Chief is a young man, and seems to exercise complete control over his "Band." . . . They acknowledge no Chief superior to the one with them. They assured me, they had never robbed the Whites, either by stealing or otherwise but ever have been and are now friendly. Col. Lander also bears testimony in their favor. This Band calls themselves Sho-sho-nees. Their haunts are Deep Creek, Raft River, and other neighboring Valleys, during the summer, all being in the neighborhood of the California Road. And during the winter, they approach the Northern settlements, and roam among them. . . . With the exception of their chief and a few of the young men, who are well provided with Blankets etc all are very destitute, many entirely naked. I gave them some presents, the first they had ever received from a Government official.

Forney summed up his report by saying of all the Indians he met along the California Trail, "They have been shot down for trivial causes. They have been robbed, and have received other ill treatment from the Whites."[3]

The next summer brought terrifying news to Agent Forney of a massacre that took place in a canyon on Sublette Cutoff, fifteen miles from the Raft River and which at first seemed to implicate Pocatello. Two Flathead Indians who had gone to an emigrant camp to trade were killed by the travelers. In response, on July 24, 1859, a party of twenty Shoshoni and Flatheads attacked the train and killed five men and one woman as well as wounding a little girl, five other men, and another woman. The raiders then took $1700, burned the four wagons, and drove off thirty horses and mules and some cattle.[4] Soon some of the stock and equipment of the train were being offered for sale by a few Shoshoni in the northern Mormon settlements of Box Elder. Forney traveled to Brigham City to investigate the affair, warned the citizens not to buy any of the stolen property, and called on General Johnston at Camp Floyd for a company of dragoons to hunt down the perpetrators of the massacre. He concluded that the murderers of the emigrants were Bannock with the help of fifteen or twenty Shoshoni from the northern valleys of Utah.[5] David D. Morgan and Richard D. Alvy from Ogden, who had been trading with emigrants near the massacre site, also reported the incident but added, "Shoshone Indians came to our camp every day; they were quiet and peaceable, and did not molest us in any manner. These Indians belonged to Chief Po-ko-tella's band."[6]

Col. Frederick W. Lander, who was camped on the Raft River about fifteen miles from City of Rocks, also learned of the attack on the emigrant train. Lander was a civil engineer who had participated in surveys for a transcontinental railroad during the 1850s and was then engaged in constructing for the army a new road to California, attempting to improve the original California Trail by building bridges and forming gentler grades for easier travel. He later distinguished himself as a brigadier general in the Union forces during the Civil War before his death on March 2, 1862.[7] Lander reported to Forney that a fourteen-year-old Indian youth, No-e-no-kook or "The Boy That Runs Fast," of "Pocatora's band of Western Snakes," came into the army camp on August 16, 1859, to report the massacre, which he said was committed by thirty warriors from the Salt Lake Snake Indians. The boy named the leader of the attackers as being Jag-e-ah or "The Man who Carries the Arrows." Others implicated were Sow-wich, "The Steam from a Cow's Belly," Ahgutch, "The Salmon," Jah-win-pooh, "The Water Goes in the Path," Jag-en-up, "The Mist after the Rain," and Wah-me-tuh-mah, "which hardly bears translation." No-e-no-kook assured Lander that Pocatello's band was not involved, "which I have little reason to doubt, as they have several times passed small parties of unarmed men, having valuable mules and horses in their possession, through their country since the treaty of last year." Here, Lander refers to a "treaty" or council meeting held with Chief Pocatello that will be described shortly.[8]

Despite the reports which came in attesting to Pocatello's friendliness and lack of implication in the massacre, when Lt. Ebenezer Gay, dispatched from Camp Floyd to apprehend the murderers, arrived at the ferry crossing of Bear River just west of Brigham City, an Indian met him who inquired which road he intended to follow. After some talk, Gay learned that the Indian was the principal chief of an encampment of fifteen lodges of Shoshoni in nearby Malad Valley and became convinced that these were the Shoshoni guilty of the emigrant murders. Placing the Indian leader in irons, Gay and forty of his soldiers started the next morning after the Indians who by this time were retreating up a canyon. Upon sight of the troops, twenty-five warriors rode out and engaged Gay's force in some long-range firing for about forty-five minutes. The Indians then withdrew and Gay abandoned any thought of pursuit. The Indian leader turned out to be Pocatello who, according to Gay, "is said by traders and others to be about the worst Indian in this country, and I am satisfied that he, with an Indian called 'Sam Pitch,' were leading Indians in the massacre."[9]

When Gay reported to his commanding officer, Maj. Isaac Lynde, at Bear River Crossing, the major released Pocatello, convinced he was not engaged in the massacre "on his promise to bring in some of the old men of the nation to have a talk."[10] Apparently Lynde wanted the opportunity to communicate with the older leaders of the Northwestern Shoshoni, perhaps uncertain about the stability and restraint of the young chief. The *Deseret News* of September 14, 1859, was outraged by the chief's release and asked, "Why was he not securely kept? and through whose agency was he permitted to escape?"

Nick Wilson, trying to recall the events of 1859, wrote that, at the time, he was telling Chief Washakie that "old Pocatello" and his "bad Indians" were involved in killing emigrants, stealing horses, and burning wagons. Wilson, despite his obvious bias against the Northwestern leader, did relate an incident in which Pocatello and some of his followers were attacked at Humboldt Springs by a party of emigrants while attempting to trade buckskins for flour. The travelers captured three of the Indian women while driving off the rest of the band. In revenge, Pocatello and his warriors followed the white men, killed all eighteen members of the party, and burned the wagons. As unreliable as Wilson's memoirs are about such events, the story nevertheless reflects the widespread perception that many western whites had about Pocatello.[11]

A more knowledgeable and objective observer of the chief and his character, in 1859, was Colonel Lander who had a unique opportunity to visit Pocatello in his camp. In a comprehensive report to the commissioner of Indian affairs concerning many of the Shoshoni tribes along the Oregon and California trails, Lander related that during his "treaty" meeting with Pocatello in 1858, the Indian leader had promised to meet the army officer near City of Rocks the following year "when the grass was beginning to dry." Lander then explained how the chief had been "ironed" by Lieutenant Gay and was unsure if "Pocataro's" band had been involved in two recent murders of emigrants. "He is a very wild and reckless chief but I am not disposed to alter my opinion of him until further light is thrown on these transactions. He has great influence in the country and we might 'better spare a better man.'"

Through the intervention of two mountaineers, Lander talked "with ten warriors, an outlying party of the band of Po-ca-taro or the 'White Plume.' The leader of these ten warriors told me that he would visit Pocataro's camp in the mountains but that the Chief's heart was bad and that he would not listen to soft words from the whites." Lander, with only a few men accompanying him, finally visited Pocatello at the Indian camp and reported that the chief

treated me and my small party with the utmost respect and consideration. I have to place on record before your department the simple fact that this young chief, known to be hostile to the whites, received me with an attention which I have seldom known manifested by the wild tribes of the interior whom I have repeatedly met, from the very fact that I had thrown myself upon his hospitality and kindness, without an escort or a large amount of presents, with full faith in the better attributes of the Indian nature. He said to me his tribe had received what he termed in the Indian language, so far as I read the interpretation "assaults of ignominy" from the white emigrants on their way to California; that one of his principal men had his squaw and his children killed by the emigrants quite recently; that the hearts of his people were very bad against the whites; that there were some things that he could not manage, and among them were the bad thoughts of his young men towards the whites on account of the deeds of the whites towards his tribe. Many of the relatives of his young men had been killed, and nothing but the death of white men could atone for this; nevertheless, I had come to him like a man, and he would meet me like a man; that his father, "Big-um," (referring to Brigham Young, of the Mormon population) had sent to him many presents, but he knew, for all that, that there was a greater man than Big-um, the Great Father of the whites, before whom Big-um was as a little finger . . . therefore, he knew and respected the power of the White Father, and that whenever he should feel certain that the White Father would treat him as well as Big-um did, then he would be the kindest friend to the Americans that they had ever known.

Lander concluded his report of the meeting with an earnest request that an appropriation be made for the purchase of presents that he could distribute to Pocatello and his people on a subsequent visit. Lander reemphasized his trust in Pocatello by telling the commissioner that after his meeting, the chief sent runners a distance of four hundred miles along the California Trail on the Humboldt to ensure safety for a party of thirteen of his engineers who were traveling to Carson Valley. But the army officer also pointed out that Johnston's troops were a hindrance to any successful conciliation of Pocatello and his band and that, during the time the chief was confined by Major Lynde, the Indian leader, "who speaks some words of English," refused to recognize a white man named James Duckworth who wanted to talk with him. Lander thought that any white men who were chosen to deal with Pocatello's band and other tribes "should possess full knowledge of the Indian character."[12]

Colonel Lander's perceptive and sensitive view of Chief Pocatello did not agree with the public attitude at that time or since. Another example of the distaste with which most chroniclers wrote about Pocatello was the fictional Almo Massacre of 1861 which never occurred but was just automatically attributed to Pocatello. In the story, a party of three hundred emigrants with sixty wagons and a number of cattle was supposedly attacked near present Almo, Idaho, just a few miles from City of Rocks. The Indians placed the emigrant train under siege for three days during which only five of the three hundred escaped and made their way to Brigham City, a hundred miles away. A relief party from the Mormon settlement reached the site of the mythical tragedy to discover the bodies of 295 people, which would have made it the greatest disaster ever visited by Indians upon any party of Americans in western history. The site of the supposed massacre was in Pocatello's home area, yet another reason for laying the fictional murders at the doorway of his tipi. [13]

Another old settler, James Bywater, in the tradition of Nick Wilson's memoirs, remembered that in the fall of 1862 a party of emigrants led by a man named Smith was also massacred at City of Rocks. The two Indian leaders involved in the "awfull butchery were Pocatello and White Beard, two most notorious cut throats and self styled chiefs. Only two of the Smith's company escaped. . . . Pocatello came in with several scalps to his waist." [14]

The incident Bywater mentioned is now known to have been just one of a number of attacks on emigrants at City of Rocks and Massacre Rocks by Pocatello and his people. By 1862, the Indian leader had concluded "that emigrant trains would have to be excluded from his lands—an area extending west of American Falls past Raft River and City of Rocks to upper Goose Creek and upper Humboldt deserts in Nevada. . . . Pocatello's band retaliated for a long sequence of attacks by emigrants, a few of whom had gone out shooting Indians along their route west through Shoshoni lands." [15] Pocatello's daughter, Jeannette Pocatello Lewis, "gave Pocatello credit for concern with heavy emigrant traffic. He finally sent his people to take away some of their wagons at Massacre Rocks." His attacks at City of Rocks was another part of his resistance to intrusion by emigrant trains. [16]

The first assaults of August occurred near City of Rocks. On August 3, according to unconfirmed reports, a Methodist train of forty persons had one man killed and lost fifteen women and children by capture. Pocatello's rampaging band then attacked a party of seven packers from the Willamette Valley three days later. One of the group was killed; the remaining six escaped with their lives but lost all their possessions. A larger party of emigrants corraled their wagons when struck at noon on August 9 near the mouth of City of Rocks canyon and fought off the Indians the rest of the day and, sporadically, all through the next night. The next morning the train escaped while the Pocatello warriors were holding a council. The whites had two of their number wounded and lost fifty head of

Attacks by Pocatello's band on emigrants passing City of Rocks were part of Pocatello's resistance to intrusion by emigrant trains. *Idaho State Historical Society.*

Massacre Rocks on the Snake River below American Falls were also the site of many attacks by Pocatello's band. *Idaho State Historical Society.*

cattle. At about the same time, perhaps on August 8, a Smith train from Warren County, Iowa, suffered a more tragic encounter when five of the party were killed and their eleven wagons and sixteen horses were taken. The survivors escaped to wander south toward the Utah settlements where some Mormons from the Box Elder area found them. The City of Rocks attacks indicated a determined effort on Pocatello's part to exclude all emigrants from his homeland. [17]

The unrelenting assaults at City of Rocks were just a prelude to a much better publicized battle which occurred over a period of two days, August 9 and 10, at Massacre Rocks, a formation of lava outcroppings on the Snake River several miles west of American Falls. Eight firsthand emigrant accounts provide a detailed description of the attacks by Pocatello's band. The first party to receive Shoshoni fire was a mule train of eight wagons and seventeen men captained by a man named Hunter. A member of the group, Charles H. Harrison later reported:

> Our hindmost wagon, . . . was suddenly attacked by some twelve or fourteen Indians. They came out of a ravine on the left of a road, and commenced the attack with bows and arrows, riding along side and shooting at the two men in the wagon, one of which was wounded in three places, but they still urged on their horses, until the Indians shot one of their animals, and by this means succeeded in stopping their teams and upsetting their wagon. The two men then left their team and ran to us, amid a perfect shower of arrows and bullets.

Hunter called on his men to ready their guns to fight for their lives, although, as Harrison wrote, "perhaps not one of us had ever been called upon to defend our lives and property by the use of such weapons." During the two-hour encounter, the emigrants "kept on firing whenever we could see an Indian, although with little hopes of hitting them, for they rode like demons, turning their horses here and there, now sitting erect in their saddles, now throwing themselves flat along their horses' backs, or completely hiding themselves behind the bodies of their ponies." Hunter and one other man were killed in this action.

An ox train of twelve wagons under George W. Adams was next to be assaulted. The Indians killed three men, mortally wounded a woman, and slightly wounded five of the other men. Three of the emigrants got "behind a bluff" and kept up a fire until the others could escape. They reported seeing "five Indians fall." Pocatello's men "took everything in the train, leaving the familiee [*sic*] that composed it entirely destitute." Most of the accounts very carefully point out that one of the men killed lost $6,000 in cash. One emigrant reported that the "seventy-five to one hundred mounted Indians" involved in the attack "would ride in on their ponies to within long range fire, and then retreat to reload." The survivors made it to the camp of a Newman-Kennedy train, which formed a corral of eighty-six wagons for the night and were soon joined by twenty more wagons under a man named Thompson.

The next morning, August 10, Captain Kennedy led a party of thirty-five well-armed men to try to recover the stock driven off by the Shoshoni five or six miles from the road, and, according to one account, they came upon about three hundred Indians, a much exaggerated figure. One eyewitness has left a more believable report:

> They come upon the Indians 20 in number with the stock—The Indians are armed with rifles which carry 200 yds & at the first fire a part of the volunteers stampede. Capt K in trying to rally them is mortally wounded—They fall back to the road where is an ox train of 10 or 12 wagons & when our informant left were trying to keep the Indians at bay.

Another emigrant gave an even less favorable picture of the stand of the untried emigrants: "At the first fire three fourths of the white men ran and the red men pursued, and after a running fight of some three miles, the Indians ceased their pursuit." Three emigrants were killed and several wounded in the battle. One man thought that nine Shoshoni had been killed, no doubt an exaggeration.

The frightening episodes at Massacre Rocks forced the separate small emigrant trains to consolidate their parties under Capt. John Walker who was in charge of forty-six wagons. By the evening of August 10, there was a reported company of 112 prepared to fight off any more attacks. The next morning, Walker selected twenty well-armed men to serve as scouts in advance of the wagons and a similar number as a rear guard. On their way to the Raft River on the night of August 11, Pocatello's band attacked the large Walker party but were driven off with no loss in personnel or stock to the emigrants. The vigilance and size of the train kept the emigrants from further assault during their travel through the rest of Pocatello's territory.

As a result of the two-day running fight at Massacre Rocks, the Shoshoni band succeeded in taking ninety head of horses, mules, and cattle; acquired about $17,500 in cash; and made off with or destroyed about $30,000 worth of wagons, provisions, and clothing. The human loss was reported as nine dead and nine wounded. One man had been scalped. It was hoped that the severely wounded Kennedy would survive. There was no Shoshoni reporter to record the Indian loss for posterity.[18]

Pocatello's well-organized and unremitting attacks at City of Rocks and Massacre Rocks in August 1862 were a forceful sign of the Indian leader's anger and frustration over the mounting emigrant intrusion into his homeland. It was a last determined effort to seek revenge for the deaths his people had incurred from the white penetration and to gain some booty in the process. His reputation as a ruthless and feared marauder was enhanced by the publicity engendered as a result of the Massacre Rocks episodes. But it was a last-gasp effort to stem the tide of white incursion. The ferocious massacre of some of his people and most of Bear Hunter's Cache Valley band by Connor's California Volunteers the following winter would bring any important Shoshoni resistance to a sudden halt.

The Northwestern Shoshoni not only had to contend with indiscriminate murders by passing emigrants but were forced also to endure longer starving periods as a result of white destruction of their grass seeds and game. The new superintendent of Indian affairs for Utah in 1862, James Duane Doty, reported to the commissioner after a winter visit to the Box Elder and Cache valley districts that "The Indians have been, in great numbers, in a starving and destitute condition. No provisions having been made for them, . . . the Indians' condition was such—with the prospect that they would rob the Mail Stations to sustain life." In the emergency, Doty charged two hundred bushels of wheat to his account and asked the commissioner to approve this unusual procedure. [19]

The superintendent was particularly concerned that the hungry bands led by Pocatello and other uncertain chieftains might descend on the settlements and demand food under threat of attack on homes and cattle herds. Knowledge that Camp Floyd had been abandoned as a result of the coming of the Civil War sharpened his worries. General Johnston and a number of troops left to join the Confederacy by August 20, 1860, when Col. Philip St. George Cooke, an officer of strong Union sentiments, took command and renamed the camp Fort Crittenden. By the fall of 1861, Cooke had sold off all the army equipment and Fort Crittenden was given back to the Mormons and the jackrabbits. With the departure of the soldiers, Utah Territory and eastern Washington Territory were left without any protection except for the Utah militia. Federal officials, including the various Indian agents, were uneasy about Mormon intentions during the Civil War and the possibility that Brigham Young and his followers might stir up the Indians against the Union and provoke attacks on emigrant parties and the transcontinental mail line. It was imperative that communication be maintained with California and the Pacific Coast. [20]

To fill the void left by the departure of the Camp Floyd troops, the secretary of war sent word to California Gov. John G. Downey, on July 24, 1861, that the government "accepts for three years one regiment of infantry and five companies of cavalry to guard the overland mail route from Carson Valley to Salt Lake and Fort Laramie." [21] To command one of the volunteer California regiments, Governor Downey appointed Col. Patrick Edward Connor, a prominent citizen of Stockton, California, and a veteran of several years in the U.S. Army, including service in the Mexican War as a captain of Texas Volunteers. [22] Connor was a feisty Irish immigrant who loved soldiering and was very good at it. He shared the suspicions and antipathies of many Americans towards Brigham Young and the Mormons and approached his task to guard the mail lines from Salt Lake City with a determination to keep the Saints as well as the Indians in check. Superintendent Doty was reassured as he watched

Col. Patrick Edward Connor came to Utah in 1861 with his California Volunteers determined to keep the Mormons as well as the Indians in check while he guarded the mail lines. *Utah State Historical Society.*

Connor and the California Volunteers took up residence at Camp Douglas
(as here seen in 1870) overlooking Salt Lake City. *Archives, Church of Jesus
Christ of Latter-day Saints.*

Connor's preparations to lead the California Volunteers to Utah and
welcomed them when they arrived in Salt Lake City on October 20,
1862, and established their headquarters at Camp Douglas on the
high bench above the city.[23]

During the trip across Nevada, Connor and his Volunteers demonstrated that there would be little discretion employed in punishing the Indian marauders they caught. At the Humboldt River,
Connor inflicted a harsh punishment on Indians who had attacked
and killed some emigrants. He ordered his troops to capture the
murderers and to "immediately hang them, and leave their bodies
thus exposed as an example of what evil-doers may expect while I
command this district." Maj. Edward McGarry, in charge of the
expedition, was further ordered to "destroy every male Indian whom
you may encounter in the vicinity of the late massacres." No prisoners were to be taken. McGarry finally killed twenty-four Indians

during this hunting expedition and sent a warning to all Shoshoni in Utah and Washington territories that retribution for misdeeds would be swift, sure, and terrible.[24] Connor and McGarry were to become Chief Pocatello's chief antagonists during the next two years.

Colonel Connor did not waste any time in engaging the Northwestern Shoshoni after his troops had settled into winter quarters at Camp Douglas. He dispatched Major McGarry to Cache Valley in November 1862 with orders to rescue a white boy held hostage by Chief Bear Hunter's band. After a two-hour bloodless battle, Bear Hunter surrendered the boy who turned out to be the half-breed son of a French mountaineer and a sister of Chief Washakie.[25] In a second more fatal engagement at Bear River Crossing in December 1862, McGarry's command shot and killed four Indian hostages when an encampment of Northwestern Shoshoni refused to give up a herd of cattle stolen from emigrants.[26] Connor and his volunteers, frustrated by not being allowed to go to the Civil War front in Virginia, were searching for an excuse to undertake a full-scale engagement with the Northwestern bands. The opportunity for battle came soon enough.

A primary cause for army and Indian officialdom's interest in northern Utah's Shoshoni affairs in 1862 was the discovery of gold on Grasshopper Creek in Dakota Territory's Beaverhead country on July 28, 1862. The event inaugurated heavy travel on the Montana Trail between Salt Lake City, the nearest base of supplies, and the new mines and took the supply trains right through Northwestern territory in Cache Valley and via the Box Elder settlements through Malad Valley.[27] The Indians resented the new intrusion and were intrigued by possibilities for plunder of the relatively small and unprotected miners' parties. Superintendent Doty, already perturbed about recent Shoshoni attacks on emigrant parties, was pleased to receive news from the commissioner that Congress had approved a $20,000 appropriation for the purpose of negotiating a treaty with the "Shoshonees or Snake Indians." The objective was not to reimburse the natives for lands already taken by whites but to give them goods and annuities so as to ensure the safety of parties traveling the Montana, Oregon, and California trails. Doty was to concentrate his efforts on those tribes considered the most dangerous to settlers and emigrants.[28] That surely included Pocatello and his band.

Before Doty had an opportunity to gather the various Shoshoni groups for treaty negotiations, a series of killings took place in Cache Valley, opening the door to Colonel Connor for a full-scale expedition against the Indians of northern Utah. News reached Salt Lake City on January 14, 1863, that two expressmen, George Clayton and Henry Bean, had been murdered on the Montana Trail in northern Cache County and that the Shoshoni of the area intended to "kill every white man they should meet with on the north side of Bear River, till they should be fully avenged" for the deaths of the four warriors killed by Major McGarry at Bear River Crossing.[29] In a second attack, a miner named John Henry Smith was killed near Bear River in Cache Valley, and, as a result, Chief Justice John F. Kinney of Utah Territory issued a warrant for the arrest of chiefs Bear Hunter, Sanpitch, and Sagwitch of the Northwestern bands in Cache Valley. Territorial Marshal Isaac L. Gibbs sought Connor's assistance in making the arrests. Connor, however, had already made plans to march north to chastize the Indians and announced that it was not his "intention to take any prisoners" but that Gibbs could accompany the expedition.[30]

Although no settler or white official was certain at the time just which Indians were involved in the Cache Valley massacre, it is interesting that in an Indian version of the events leading to the Bear River Massacre and an account of the "battle" itself, the author, Mae T. Parry, a descendant of one of the participants, credits members of Pocatello's band as being the assailants. In her "Massacre at Boa Ogoi," Parry names three Indians who had stolen horses and cattle from Mormon farmers during the month of January: One-eye Tom, Zee coo chee (Chipmunk), and Qua ha da do coo wat (Lean or Skinny Antelope). The killings of Clayton, Bean, and Smith took place shortly after this incident. Parry then notes, "These Indians were not from the Northwestern Shoshone group but had come from Chief Pocatello's band."[31] Apparently some of today's Shoshoni have the same perception whites of the time had of Pocatello—the leader of a wily, dangerous, and destructive group of Indians.

With a warrant issued for the arrest of Bear Hunter and the other chiefs and with his plans matured, Colonel Connor set out for a large encampment of Shoshoni located on Beaver Creek where that stream enters Bear River about twelve miles northwest of the small Mormon settlement of Franklin, now in Idaho. There were probably about 450 Indians in the village—men, women, and children—on January 29, 1863, when Connor and his California Volunteers attacked the camp. Parry, in her account, explains that for a week or two prior to Connor's assault, there were a great many more Shoshoni at the village, who gathered to visit and participate in the annual Warm Dance held to "drive out the cold." Among the visitors were members of Washakie's Eastern Shoshoni and "Chief Pocatello's band." Because the Indians were aware of the approach of the Connor troops, the day before the massacre took place, Pocatello and part of his people and the Eastern Shoshoni left the camp and escaped the conflict, but some Pocatello Indians remained and became victims of the California troops. In the four-hour engagement on the morning of January 29,[32] Connor's men killed about 250 of the Shoshoni men, women, and children, including Chief Bear Hunter, while suffering 23 casualties. The affair started out as a battle and ended in a slaughter of the Indians.[33] Chief Sagwitch escaped the conflict with only a wound in his hand and led some of the freezing warriors to the "friendly lodge" of Pocatello who was then encamped about twenty miles north in Malad Valley.[34] The "Battle of Bear River," as it has been called in western history, has been ignored by many historians, although it resulted in more Indian deaths than other better-reported engagements. Five years after the affair, one *Deseret News* reporter visited the scene of the battlefield and discovered "The bleached skeletons of scores of noble red men" still ornamenting the grounds. He expressed regret that Pocatello and his "gang" had not also been annihilated in the fray.[35]

Newly promoted Brigadier General Connor was determined to pursue and punish the Shoshoni who had escaped the battle and wrote in his report of the engagement, "The chiefs Pocatello and San Pitch, with their bands of murderers, are still at large. I hope to be able to kill or capture them before spring. If I succeed, the Overland

Route west of the Rocky Mountains will be rid of the bedouins who have harassed and murdered emigrants on that route for a series of years."[36] That it was necessary to mount an expedition to go after Pocatello and other dissident Shoshoni leaders seemed clear to Mormon settlers in northern Utah. Samuel Roskelley wrote that the neighboring Indians had told him they were "so angry with the soldiers" they intended to steal all the horses and cattle they could and meant "to kill every white man they could find."[37]

Rumors began circulating in March 1863 that Connor was preparing an expedition to go into the Fort Hall area to look for the rebellious chieftains and their bands. The *Sacramento Union* of March 2, 1863, expressed the thought that Pocatello could "derive no aid or comfort" from the news and that the chief "may rest assured that if P. Ed. Connor ever gets his eyes upon him and his band 'he's a *gone* coon.'" The editor opined that in two weeks the weather would have moderated enough so that the troops could get underway but would not have improved enough "to set Po-ca-tello a-roaming." A rumor was also deliberately started that the California Volunteers were to be sent to the eastern front of the Civil War to "keep Po-ca-tello from learning the kindness in store for him," as the soldiers made preparations to hunt him down. The *Sacramento Union* of April 4, 1863, echoed these belligerent statements: "There can be no hesitation on following up the fighting policy till Pocatello and his band of marauders are wiped out. They must be killed or driven." With such notices in prominent California newspapers, Chief Pocatello was gaining notoriety as a prominent and recalcitrant Indian leader.

Reports from the Montana mines began reaching Salt Lake City with rumors about Pocatello's movements. Expressman A. H. Conover came in from Bannack City with the news that the Shoshoni chief was then in the vicinity of the Portneuf River and "wants to fight, and would be glad to have Gen. Connor send out an expedition in that direction, that he may have a chance to gratify his greediness for glory."[38] Further speculation had Pocatello stealing stock from south of the Snake River in the Fort Hall area.[39] The Salt Lake City reporter for the *Sacramento Union* issue of May 30, 1863, asserted that Pocatello had been killed at Bear River, as attested by Chief Washakie, and that the Mormons were trying to "keep alive the impression that he was still sound in the flesh." The scribe then attacked the Saints for inciting the Indians and supplying them with powder and lead and charged that it was well known that Bear Hunter and Pocatello had had only to demand flour and the Mormon farmers would immediately supply it even though they knew the Indians were at war with the federal government.

Connor finally set out on his northern expedition on May 6, 1863, to establish an outlying garrison at Camp Connor, the site of present Soda Springs, Idaho, and to attempt to capture the Shoshoni who had escaped him at Bear River. He did not find Pocatello, who apparently had moved to the headwaters of the Green River to escape the troops "where it is hoped that he will remain for a long time to come," according to the *Deseret News* of June 3, 1863. Connor was back in Salt Lake City by May 30 and Superintendent Doty, who accompanied the general, reported that the Bannock and Shoshoni he met were friendly, especially in the presence of Connor's dragoons, and that "The only bands that appear determined to continue hostilities were those of Pokatelo, Sagowitz, and Sanpitz— and with these I could obtain no communication. They must be left to Genl Connor's troops."[40]

Despite his pessimistic forecast, Doty went ahead with his efforts to sign treaties with the major segments of the Shoshoni Nation. With the help of Agent Luther Mann he negotiated an agreement with Washakie and the Eastern Shoshoni at Fort Bridger on July 2, 1863.[41] Then, the unexpected occurred. Four days after his meeting with Washakie, Doty wired the commissioner, "Pokatelle sends word that he wishes to treat for peace. Sanritz and Sagoity have fled north of Snake River."[42] Mormon Bishop Alvin Nichols of Brigham City confirmed the fact by writing Doty on July 11 of the situation concerning Pocatello,

a portion of whose band has been in this city lately; led by one George, consisting of nine lodges, bringing intelligence that they wish for peace and that Pocatello is willing to give ten horses to prove that he is sincere, he wishes to be at peace with the whites says the emigrants shall travel through the country without any molestation to them or their property by any of his men. Likewise he would be glad to meet with you and make peace but he is afraid to come to Salt Lake City lest he should meet with any of the soldiers who not understanding his business would kill him. They are in very destitute circumstances.[43]

Finally, General Connor, on July 18, passed the word to the commander of his army district that "I have received a message from Pocatello, the celebrated Snake chief, begging for peace and asking for a conference. He says he is tired of war, and has been effectually driven from the Territory with a small remnant of his once powerful band. He now sues for peace, and having responded favorably to his request I will meet him at an early day, and will conclude with him what I have no doubt will prove a lasting peace."[44]

With these assurances, Connor and Doty met with nine Northwestern band leaders at Box Elder on July 30, 1863, and concluded the Treaty of Box Elder. There were five articles: (1) friendly relations were to be "re-established" between the United States and the bands of the "Shoshonee Nation," (2) the chiefs agreed to all the provisions of the Treaty of Fort Bridger of July 2, which included Indian promises that routes of travel and settlements would be ensured safety; that telegraph, stage, and railroad stations could be located in Northwestern territory; and that the Shoshoni would claim no more interest in their homelands than they had had under Mexican law; (3) the United States agreed to pay the bands a sum of $5,000 a year for a term of twenty years as compensation for the destruction of game by white travelers along the western trails plus $2,000 at the time of signing the treaty "to relieve their immediate necessities"; (4) "The country claimed by Pokatello, for himself and his people is bounded on the west by Raft River and on the east by the Portneuf Mountains"; and (5) a reiteration about land claims under Mexico.[45]

"Pokatello" signed the treaty first as the most prominent leader. He was followed by the marks made by Toomontso, Sanpitz, Tosowitz, Yahnoway, Weerahsoop, Pahragoosahd, Tahkwetoonah, and Omashee (John Pokatello's brother). Chief Sagwitch was unable to affix his mark because he was shot by "some fiends" while a prisoner of the California Volunteers. The chief was on his way to the treaty negotiations when a detachment of troops captured him in Box Elder Canyon. Although seriously wounded, he eventually re-

Two views of the Shoshoni Pocatello band. *Archives, Church of Jesus Christ of Latter-day Saints; Marriott Library, University of Utah.*

covered and accepted the terms of the treaty along with the other Indian leaders.[46]

Superintendent Doty and General Connor recognized Pocatello as the most important of the Northwestern chiefs by designating the exact boundaries of his homeland, an acknowledgment that his band roamed beyond the limits of Mormon settlement which had swallowed up the other Northwestern lands. To complete his year of peacemaking, Doty concluded agreements with the Western Shoshoni at Ruby Valley, Nevada Territory, on October 1, 1863; the Gosiute Shoshoni at "Tuilla" Valley, Utah Territory, on October 2, 1863; and the mixed bands of Bannock and Shoshoni at Soda Springs, Idaho Territory, on October 14, 1863.[47] In a summary of his year's activities, Doty reemphasized the importance of the Treaty of Box Elder, "the first object was to effect and secure a peace with Pokatello, as the road to Beaver Head gold mines and those on Boise river, as well as the northern California and southern Oregon roads, pass through his country."[48]

By the summer of 1864, Chief Pocatello, now at peace with the whites, was well known to the readers of many western newspapers and certainly the government Indian officials, army officers, and the Saints of Utah. Peter Maughan, one of the prominent Mormon leaders in Cache Valley, could proudly report to Brigham Young on July 28, 1864, "Pokatello took dinner at my home yesterday. this is his first visit to see the Mormons in Cache we give him a sack of flour and sent him on his way rejoicing giving us the appearance of another visit with his tribe at some future time. these are all good Indians."[49]

Just across the mountains in the Bear Lake region, another Mormon colonizer, Charles C. Rich, also had a meeting with the now-famous chief but with a different outcome. Rich agreed to give Pocatello a steer from the local herd but stipulated that one particular animal could not be chosen because it was the only one owned by a poor man. Pocatello stubbornly insisted on this animal and threatened to kill it whereupon Rich dragged the Indian leader from his horse, and for a moment the two powerful men confronted each other. Then, in a gesture of mock good nature, the chief slapped Rich on the back and said, "You heap big white chief." Pocatello chose another steer, according to Rich's biographer.[50]

While Mormon leaders were enjoying a congenial relationship with Pocatello during 1864, General Connor engaged the chief in a very serious confrontation. Ben Holladay, the "Stagecoach King," had established his Overland Stage Line on the route between Salt Lake City and the Montana mines, and his assistant superintendent, Paul Coburn, had something upsetting to report. During an inspection trip of the line, Coburn learned from his terror-stricken employees at Malad Spring Station that Pocatello had been there and had appropriated most of the food supplies. Apparently other members of the band had also gotten in the habit of stopping off for free food at the station. At the Elk Horn stop, Coburn encountered Pocatello who had already taken some flour and had ordered the stocktender's wife to prepare a meal for him. Confronting the chief, Coburn asked if he was now expecting to collect "tithing along the Stage Line." Pocatello simply replied, "Yes." Outraged by his brazenness, Coburn returned to Salt Lake City two days later and made a formal complaint to Capt. Charles H. Hempstead, post marshal at Camp Douglas. When told of the incident, General Connor was even angrier and ordered Pocatello's arrest without even informing O. H. Irish, the superintendent of Indian affairs for Utah.[51]

But the news got around, and when Irish checked with Captain Hempstead, he was told "that Gen. Connor had set to arrest Pocatello, and that he would try him, and if guilty of the offences charged in the affidavit,—he would hang him." Connor was unmoved by Irish's statement that Pocatello had been allowed to proceed through the Mormon towns unmolested on his way to talk to the Indian superintendent about the recent Treaty of Box Elder.[52]

The army newspaper, *The Daily Union Vedette* of October 27, 1863, described the interrogation of Pocatello which had taken place the day before:

> Latterly, serious charges have been preferred against Pocatello—to the effect that he has been visiting the stage stations this side of Snake River—demanding under threats—provisions and whatever he wanted; and generally depredating all along the Malade river. Gen.

Connor, accordingly, a few days since sent a detachment under Capt.
[J. W.] Calder, Nevada Volunteers, who captured the renowned Chief
near Box Elder, and brought him in arrest to Camp Douglas.

At the examination yesterday, there were present besides Gen.
Connor and members of his staff, Governor Doty, Col. Irish, Superintendent of Indian affairs, and Ben Holladay, Esq. Dimick Huntington
acted as interpreter. The charges were stated to Pocatello, and reference had to the treaty. The Indian Chief with the most supreme indif-
ference listened calmly, and then demanded to know who "told Connor all this." The proofs were rehearsed to him. But he seemed to be a
pretty good Constitutional lawyer, and declined pertinaciously to an-
swer "any question tending to criminate himself." He denied most
positively having this season been on the Malade, insisting that he had
ranged all the time between Box Elder and Cache Valley.

Gen. Connor then informed Pocatello that he would send a commissioned officer to take further testimony, and if the charges were not
sustained he would release him and compensate him fully for his arrest
and detention; but if proven to be true, he would send Pocatello back
to his country where he had murdered so many whites, and there
erecting a gallows, hang him between Heaven and earth—a warning
to all bad Indians. Col. Irish, previously, had stated to Pocatello that
the Indian goods had arrived, but would not be distributed to
Pocatello's band until this matter was finally settled. To a suggestion
that Pocatello should be tried by the civil authorities, Gen. Connor
feelingly remarked, that more than twenty of his soldiers were buried
within sight, killed by this murderer and his band, and he should take
the sole responsibility of punishing him if guilty.

Pocatello was then remanded to the guard house to await further
investigation.

In his report of the hearing, Irish informed the commissioner that
Pocatello had not been involved in the fighting at Bear River at all
and that Connor certainly had his revenge for the soldiers he had lost
"by killing as he reports some hundreds of Indians." Irish concluded
that Connor would be going too far to execute Pocatello even if all
the charges against the chief were sustained.[53]

The next day Irish put in writing his strong objections to any
thought of lethal punishment for Pocatello. He told Connor that
there was a good possibility of a general outbreak by the Shoshoni
should their chief be hanged. Furthermore, if Pocatello had demanded food it was because a negligent government had been late in
delivering the annuity goods to the Northwestern bands under their

treaty. Irish was particularly critical that the general would take "the sole responsibility of the arrest, trial, and if he be found guilty of the offences charged, of the punishment of the Chief Pocatello."[54] Irish repeated his complaints to the commissioner and again warned that an Indian war was likely if Pocatello were executed. Irish had even offered to compensate the Holladay stage company for the supplies taken by the Indians, but the gesture had been refused as being "too trifling."[55]

Ben Holladay then closed the affair by writing General Connor "that the alleged Offences of 'Pocatello' are not of that serious character he at first apprehended and understood them to be and requests that no further action be taken by me." Connor received the letter on November 4. The proprietor of the Overland Stage Line had apparently underestimated Connor and knew the Overland Company would face wholesale attacks on its stations should the ruthless general carry through his promise and the Shoshoni respond as they were threatening to do. Connor indicated he was going to transfer the prisoner to Irish for the superintendent's action.[56] A relieved Irish reemphasized to the commissioner on November 9: "The Northern Bands of the Shoshonies upon learning of Genl Connors intention of hanging 'Pocatello' had gone to the Mountains with an intention of preparing for war. . . . If the Military authorities will allow me to manage these Indians without any further interference, I am satisfied that by a judicious use of the appropriations made I can maintain peace." Irish released Pocatello at once and sent him to Box Elder with instructions to gather his people for a council meeting to be held there the following week.[57]

The Northwestern bands met at Box Elder in mid-November with James Duane Doty, recently named governor of the Utah Territory, and Irish, who distributed the annuity goods and received their approval of the revised treaty which had been amended to include the provision concerning land titles under the laws of Mexico. Irish reported "These [Indians] have in times past been the most troublesome Indians in this Superintendency, they now seem remarkably well disposed toward the Government. My successful Efforts on behalf of Pocatello has had a most Salutary Effect and I apprehend no further difficulties with them.[58]

Because Commissioner of Indian Affairs William T. Dole did not receive the letter from Irish with an enclosure of the letter from the Overland Stage Line reporting Pocatello's release by Connor until November 25, the commissioner had decided to take immediate action to save the life of an Indian chief who might be hanged at any time by a ruthless and impatient army commander. In a hasty letter to Secretary of the Interior John P. Usher, he outlined the problem and concluded, "I respectfully ask your immediate interference in behalf of this unfortunate, though perhaps guilty chief, to the extent that you will request the President to telegraph to General Connor, directing him to delay the execution of Pocatello, if found guilty, until the papers in this case have been submitted to your Department, and all the facts thoroughly investigated."[59]

Secretary Usher visited President Abraham Lincoln that same day. After reading the correspondence from Superintendent Irish, the president issued orders to the secretary of war that the chief was not to be executed and a telegram with that message was sent to Utah. Dole wrote Irish on November 26, 1864, giving him the particulars of Lincoln's decision.[60] Ben Holladay had, of course, already withdrawn his charges against Pocatello and Connor had already released the chief to Superintendent Irish, but officials in Washington were unaware of these developments in Utah when they took this humanitarian action. With all of his responsibilities in conducting a war to save the Union, Abraham Lincoln found time to save the life of an Indian chief far out in the Great Basin.

The seven years from 1857 to 1864 were significant in transforming Pocatello from a little-known leader of a band of four hundred Northwestern Shoshoni to one of the most noted Indian chiefs of the Great Basin and Snake River regions. After the tumultuous events of these years, Pocatello faced a new set of circumstances as railroads and a reservation at Fort Hall changed his life and those of his followers.

5

A Reservation and a Railroad

The promise of the United States to the Northwestern Shoshoni that the government would allocate $5,000 a year for food and supplies for the bands opened a new chapter in their history. It wasn't much but both Indian leaders and Indian agents trusted it would be sufficient to get the tribes through the starving period each winter until further provisions could be made to settle the natives on some land and help them to become farmers. But the next decade proved even more frustrating and precarious as Congress failed to appropriate funds (which were insufficient anyway) and transportation difficulties delayed the distribution of annuities. Pocatello and his people were to be caught in this deteriorating situation along with the other Shoshoni groups.

Some of the Shoshoni refused to accept the hit-or-miss efforts of the government to help feed them and began plundering the Overland Stage Line stations. Furthermore, at least a few of these raiders found it convenient to blame Pocatello for their assaults. Paul Coburn, still in charge of the Holladay lines north of Salt Lake City, complained to Superintendent Irish in April 1865 that "Indians representing themselves to be subjects of Pocatello an Indian Chief of your District are constantly committing depredations on the Overland Stage Line, carrying the U.S. Mails between S. L. City Utah & Walla Wall Wash Territory." The marauders were running off stock, stealing provisions from the posts, and sometimes actually taking possession of the stations after driving out the agents and stocktenders. Most of the attacks took place along the Snake River and near the Salmon Falls Ferry, quite a distance from Pocatello's homeland and within the jurisdiction of the new Idaho Territory recently established on March 4, 1863.[1]

Irish answered Coburn by pointing out that he should request aid from the governor of Idaho who was ex officio superintendent of Indian affairs for the new territory and that the guilty parties were probably the mixed bands of Shoshoni and Bannock from the Fort Hall area and not the much-maligned Pocatello. He recommended that instead of sending a military force to punish the attackers that provisions be distributed to the starving natives who were killing and eating the horses and mules taken from the stations. Irish promised to help with food supplies but urged that Coburn petition Idaho officials for help.[2]

Acting then on his own responsibility, Coburn hired Mormon guide Dimick Huntington and William Mann to search the northern trails, to learn who the miscreants were, and to capture them. Reaching Portneuf Canyon, Huntington came upon Pocatello and hired the chief and three of his men to help in tracking the robbers. The combined posse searched the trails for two days without success. Heavy rains had obliterated the tracks, "but the wolves had left their lair." Abandoning the pursuit, Huntington returned to Salt Lake City to report "Po-ca-tello as more than willing to render all the assistance he could." The chief seemed anxious to prove that he and his followers were not to blame for the attacks. The common belief that he spent twenty-four hours every day scheming how to make life miserable for all whites simply was not true.[3]

While probably not involved in the depredations on the mail line, Pocatello and his Northwestern friends waited impatiently for their 1865 annuity goods, which were snowbound four hundred miles away. Irish wrote the commissioner on October 9 that if they did not arrive within a few days he would be forced to buy supplies from the local merchants and repay them with the provisions when they did come.[4] Fortunately, the "presents" showed up in time for allocation by the first of November. Irish, accompanied by Gov. Charles Durkee, met about six hundred of the Northwestern Shoshoni at Box Elder. The Indians "received their presents with much satisfaction."[5] This was the beginning of an annual event which usually was held along lower Bear River just west of Brigham City until the mid-1870s by which time many of the bands had left to become residents of the new Fort Hall Reservation. Pocatello and his group participated in most of these annual give aways, and the chief was no doubt also pleased with the appointment on December 10, 1865, of A. G. Turner as special agent for the Indians at the Goose Creek Mountains, very near Pocatello's home country.[6]

From the signing of the Treaty of Box Elder in the summer of 1863 to the late 1870s, Pocatello's band and the other Northwestern Shoshoni lived precariously, traveling wherever they could to find food. Utah Indian Supt. F. H. Head reported to the commissioner in September 1866 that about eighteen hundred Northwestern Shoshoni were led by three principal chiefs: "Pokatello, Black Beard, and San Pitz." Head indicated that Pocatello and Black Beard had joined Washakie for his annual buffalo hunt in the Wind River Valley, returning to Utah in May 1867. Washakie's acceptance of the two Northwestern chiefs was a recognition that they and their people were sufficiently outfitted with good horses, had the skills necessary to hunt the buffalo, and, above all, could be counted on as trustworthy warriors against enemy Plains tribes who nearly always contested ownership of the dwindling herds of bison. The superintendent pointed out that the $5,000 annuity was sufficient to clothe the Shoshoni groups but not enough to sustain them during the winter months. None of them had yet "displayed any inclination to agriculture."[7]

The leader of the Saints in Utah was pleased that the federal government partially relieved his people of the responsibility for feeding the Northwestern bands. Brigham Young's Manuscript History reported on March 11, 1866, "President Young said as the Lamanites are hostile, let us exercise faith about them and learn what the will of the Lord is. Let us send our Interpreters to them and make presents and tell [them] they must stop fighting. It is better to give them $5000 than have to fight and kill them for they are of the House of Israel."[8] But the Northwestern Shoshoni did not always receive the entire $5,000 annuity. In the fall of 1866, Head distributed a portion of it to the "mixed bands" at Fort Hall, Shoshoni and Bannock whose own Treaty of Soda Springs had not been ratified and who therefore were desperate for food.[9] It is little wonder that Pocatello led his people in search of Wyoming buffalo, especially when the valuable robes they procured could be sold in the settlements for high prices.[10]

Superintendent Head attempted to keep Pocatello and his fellow chiefs supplied with the necessary articles for their nomadic way of life, recognizing that it might be some time before the wandering bands would agree to settle down and be farmers. On January 4, 1868, he gently chided the commissioner for sending beaver traps attached to chains so weak that the animals easily broke them and dragged the traps away. He explained, "The beaver is a very strong animal." Also, he asked the Office of Indian Affairs to provide the Indians with brass kettles instead of iron ones because the latter were "too cumbersome" for travel and were "also soon worn out." The Shoshoni usually traded them off for brass kettles at the ratio of four to one.[11] Head was gratified that when he gave the "most reliable chiefs" fifteen cows to encourage entry into ranching, the Indian leaders kept them as breeding animals and had not eaten them when Head visited the bands a little later. Pocatello might not have been one of the "reliable" chiefs.[12]

Some of the Mormon farmers were not as amiable about feeding the Indians as was the Mormon prophet. J. C. Wright of Brigham City wrote the *Deseret News* on September 15, 1868, quite critical of the Treaty of Box Elder when "six or eight little one-horse-power, self-made chiefs—the biggest rowdies, robbers and rascals in the whole nation, walked up to the scratch and signed the document. The names of those who signed the declaration on the part of the nation were Sagwitch, Sanpitch, Black Beard, Pocatello." Wright then described the annual distribution of presents on lower Bear River near Brigham City when about six hundred Northwestern Shoshoni arrived to "pitch their lodges as near fields of grain, potatoes and melon patches as they can, and then commence their business of begging and stealing." He estimated that Box Elder County citizens each year lost 1,500 bushels of wheat to the scavenging natives worth $3,000, 500 bushels of corn at $750, and $1,000 worth of oats, barley, squash, and potatoes plus cattle and horses taken to the tune of a total of $8,000. Wright proposed that the farmers of his county would be better off to pay the North-western Indians $5,000 "out of our own pockets" to keep the natives away from Box Elder. Of course, Wright conveniently failed to mention that the Indians were there long before the whites ever moved in.

Another settler, Joseph C. Rich of Paris, Idaho, in the Bear Lake region, belligerently harped back to Colonel Connor's battle with Bear Hunter at Bear River. Writing the *Deseret News* of May 20, 1868, he reported that when he visited the battlefield on his way to Salt Lake City, the "bleached skeletons" were still on the site and that he could almost feel "the influence of the departed still hanging around the battle field. I am sorry to say Po-co-tello and his small 'gang' were not identified in this conflict."[13]

With even the easier-to-feed-than-to-fight Mormons exasperated by the constant begging visits of the Northwestern Shoshoni, the government began to take heed of requests from Indian agents of the territories of Utah, Wyoming, and Idaho that a reservation must be found for the wandering tribes to keep them away from the settlements and to provide farms for them. By 1868, most government officials had agreed on a site at Fort Hall where the Blackfoot and Portneuf rivers meet the Snake River. Governor David W. Ballard of Idaho was the chief mover and had already gotten that area established as a Boise Shoshoni reservation on June 14, 1867, but it was the conclusion of the Treaty of Fort Bridger of July 3, 1868, with the Eastern Shoshoni and Bannock which finally assigned the Fort Hall reserve to Fort Hall Shoshoni and Bannock. In addition to them, it was to become the home for the Boise and Bruneau bands, and eventually the Northwestern and Lemhi, although the latter refused to move to Fort Hall until 1907. For Pocatello and other Northwestern leaders, it was a gradual process until the mid-1870s when they finally drifted into Fort Hall to make it their permanent home.[14]

While the process of establishing the Fort Hall reserve was under way, on May 8, 1868, B. F. White, a prominent citizen of Malad, Idaho, and later governor of Montana, wrote Governor Ballard urging speedy action to set up the new Indian home. White had met Chief Tahgee of the Bannock during the fall of 1867 and reported that the tribe expected to settle at Fort Hall during the summer of 1868. White continued:

> "Pocatello" with about 300 Indians, large & small are encamped in Cache Valley about 40 miles from this place, and are making calculations on going on to the Reservation. They will probably be along here in a few days.
>
> Of the Bannacks there probably need be no fear as they have always been very peaceably inclined but Pocatello and his band are known to be very bad Indians and their name is allmost a terror to the inhabitants of northern Utah. With their present force if they should take the notion they would clean out this entire country. [15]

White would have been relieved to know that Special Agent Charles F. Powell was already taking the necessary steps to get the new reservation into operation. In late December 1868, Powell finally traveled from Boise to Fort Hall on an inspection trip to learn which tribes along the Snake River could be persuaded to move to the reservation and to look over the site. [16] At Malad, he met some of Pocatello's people where they were camped and engaged in hunting and fishing. He learned that Pocatello and a portion of the band were with Chief Tahgee and the Bannock in the Wind River country. Powell gave the Malad encampment a small amount of flour, explained that they should plan to move to the reservation in the spring and received assurances that "they would join me at Fort Hall early in the Spring. They appear to be very well disposed Indians, and I doubt not will be only too glad to be permanently located." [17]

On April 26, 1869, Powell wrote from Fort Hall that he had successfully moved most of the Boise and Bruneau Shoshoni from the Boise area to the reservation and, with the Shoshoni and a few Bannock on the ground also, was beginning to plow a few acres to get a farm going. Tahgee and Pocatello had still not returned from the buffalo country. [18] B. F. White was no doubt pleased with this information and hoped that now the terrible Pocatello might agree to settle down under the auspices of a government Indian agent.

The Mormon settlers of the Bear Lake region had watched Pocatello move through their valley on his way back from Wind River shortly before White observed them in Cache Valley. John A. Hunt of Rich County reported to church leaders in Salt Lake City that grain was in plentiful supply at Bear Lake "and no doubt will continue so if Pokatello and his band do not stop in the valley too long—they are there at present.[19] The editor of the *Deseret News* of June 2, 1869, expanded on this theme: "Po-ca-tello, the renowned Indian warrior, whose reputation for honesty is almost as great as that of a Congressman, had paid a begging visit to the settlements without stealing anything from the settlers: The definition of the word Po-ca-tello, in English, literally rendered means 'give-us-another-sack-of-flour-and-two-beeves.' "

By late June, Tahgee and five hundred of his Bannock tribe were at the reservation demanding an end to the "promise after promise made to them" and a final resolution of whether they were to have a part of the Fort Hall reserve for their home. President Ulysses S. Grant's action in signing an executive order of July 30, 1869, settled the matter by placing the Bannock at Fort Hall. Chief Tahgee was an impressive and strong Indian leader who commanded the respect of his followers as well as every white official who met him. Agent Luther Mann of Wyoming thought that Tahgee was "a most reliable and excellent Indian, and to his prudent counsels the moderation and patient endurance of broken faith by this tribe is due."[20]

Pocatello and two hundred of his band also appeared at the reservation at the same time as Tahgee. Powell reported of Pocatello's group, "They wanted presents I supplied them with flour and bacon from my limited stores . . . They say come and 'talk' with us so that we may know what you wish of us." Both Tahgee and Pocatello were anxious to be settled permanently at Fort Hall because on their winter's venture after buffalo in the Wind River area they had been attacked by the Sioux and had lost twenty-nine warriors in the ensuing battle. But with twelve hundred hungry Indians at Fort Hall and only "limited stores," Agent Powell faced an impossible situation. The two Indian leaders demanded a talk with some "Big Chief."[21] The *Idaho Statesman* at Boise could report on July 15, 1869, that a large number of some old neighbors, the Boise Shoshoni, were back at that city having left the reservation due to "a scarcity of rations." The pleasing prospects of a permanent home at Fort Hall were already withering in the summer sun. Powell escaped his personal dilemma of too many Indians and not enough food when Lt. William H. Danilson took over as full-time agent on July 30, 1869.[22]

The Utah supervisor of Indian affairs was pleased that the Fort Hall Reservation was now a reality. Superintendent J. E. Tourtellotte reported to the commissioner on December 3, 1869, that the Northwestern Shoshoni were much less inclined to agriculture than the other tribes within his jurisdiction, and, anyway, had much better hunting grounds. He did not know of any desirable farming land in Utah not already occupied by the whites that could be irrigated without great government expense.[23] Chief Pocatello had apparently already decided that Fort Hall was the only possibility for a permanent home but, nevertheless, continued to be present at the annual distribution of food and provisions on the lower Bear River every fall.

Pocatello's continual wanderings through the Mormon settlements of Northern Utah made him the target of accusations whenever any dastardly incident occurred that might be attributed to Indians. A case in point was the abduction by some Indians of G. W. Thurston's four-year-old daughter in Cache Valley. The father advertised widely in the *Deseret News* and other papers, offering a reward of five thousand dollars to anyone who would rescue the girl from her captors. He learned that "Pocatello had confessed the theft and that they sold her to a white man on Salmon River."[24] According to this story, the chief had admitted the theft to church leader Peter Maughan, who now wrote the *Deseret News* to give the facts in the case. Maughan reported that a month after the kidnapping, Chief "Sige-Witch" had informed him that he had heard that "Poka-tel-lo's" stepmother had stolen the "Mormon papoose." On May 19, 1869, Pocatello admitted to Maughan that he believed an Indian named Yam-bi-ah and an Indian woman named Tic-a-man had stolen the child and traded her to a white man on the Salmon River. Then, Chief Black Beard revealed to Maughan that Tic-a-man was really Pocatello's stepmother and that she had left Pocatello's father and "ran off with another Indian . . . to the mines, on very disreputable business." Maughan thought the child might still be alive. He then defended the practice of the Mormons in feeding the natives to avoid an Indian war and "through a sense of humanity, realizing that they look upon the very lands we occupy as a portion of their inheritance, . . . should it really be proved that a vagabond among the red men has stolen a white child, let us look at the catalogue of crimes perpetrated by the whites themselves, and ask who should cast the first stone."[25] It was perhaps understandable that when Maughan died in 1871, a number of Indians attended his funeral. Perhaps Pocatello was among them. One native mourner is reported to have said, "Our father has gone and he never had two tongues."[26] The most interesting part of the incident for this story is the reference to Pocatello's father who might still have been alive at the time. The little Thurston girl was never found.

The year 1869 marked the entry of a new element into the lives of Pocatello's tribe with the completion of the transcontinental railroad, the golden spike at Promontory Summit having been driven right in the heart of his country. The Central Pacific immediately established a freight transfer point for the Boise mines at Kelton, just north of Great Salt Lake and next door to Pocatello's aboriginal village, Biagamugep. The little station was soon thronged with freight wagons and stagecoaches and all of the services necessary to support the operations. For over a decade, until the completion of the Oregon Short Line from Pocatello Station in the 1880s made Kelton a ghost town, it was a busy place and probably played host to a number of Pocatello's people, although no documentation exists to tell the story.[27]

For freight and passengers going from the Central Pacific to the Beaverhead country by way of the Montana Trail, however, there is a lot of evidence to describe Indian-white relations at the new freight-transfer point at Corinne, Utah. A group of gentile (non-Mormon) businessmen from Salt Lake City and some former Union army officers founded this town about six miles west of Brigham City in March 1869. It was composed almost wholly of gentile citizens and served as a marshalling point during its ten-year existence as a commercial hub for goods and passengers to Montana. The town never boasted of a population of more than a thousand permanent residents, but it had a newspaper which delighted in attacking the Mormons and which tried, unsuccessfully, to break Brigham Young's political and economic hold on Utah. With the completion of the Utah and Northern Railroad to Marsh Valley in Idaho by 1878, the traffic from Corinne by freight wagons and stagecoaches was cut off, the non-Mormons fled the town, and Mormon farmers moved in to take possession. It has been a Mormon village ever since.

For Pocatello's people and other Northwestern Shoshoni, Corinne was important because the town was located on the west bank of the Bear River just a short distance above its confluence with Great Salt Lake and within two or three miles of a traditional winter camp of the Shoshoni, especially for the band headed by Chief Sagwitch. Furthermore, this place came to be the site where the Utah Indian agents distributed the Northwestern annuity goods every fall, and Pocatello and his tribe were nearly always in attendance with the possible exception of the years when he was hunting buffalo in Wyoming with Washakie and Tahgee. This annual event and the daily comings and goings of various Shoshoni groups who camped near the town received constant attention from local newspaper editors.[28]

Most of the articles in the town's press about the Shoshoni, who visited Corinne almost daily from their nearby Bear River camp, were concerned with their "filthy" habits and presented a strong racial bias, a marked contrast to the friendlier tone adopted by Utah's Mormons. The newspapers took notice especially of the destitution and "biting hunger" of the Indians. The editors made little attempt to rally the citizens of the town to help the starving Shoshoni. Instead, the newswriters just attacked Indian officials for not taking care of their charges.[29]

While the Corinnethians, as they liked to call themselves, were berating Indian agents and ridiculing the Shoshoni in 1870, Mormon leaders continued their policies of feeding and befriending the natives. Brigham Young and other leaders tried to counteract government suspicions about Mormon instigation of Indian attacks. Lt. G. M. Fleming, agent for the Eastern Shoshoni in Wyoming, wrote Governor J. A. Campbell of that territory on June 14, 1870, that Young had supposedly offered Chief Washakie provisions, horses, and presents if the Indian leader would "join the Mormons against

Corinne, Utah, was founded by a group of non-Mormon businessmen and became an important commercial center for traffic on the Montana Trail. It was also located within two or three miles of a traditional winter camp of the Shoshoni. *Utah State Historical Society.*

the gentiles and soldiers this year." Fleming reported this was the reason for an assemblage of about two thousand Shoshoni and Ute Indians then at Bear Lake.[30]

Four days later, a resident of the Bear Lake district, L. L. Pohnanteer, signed an affidavit giving his version of why the Indians were gathered at the lake. He reported that Chief Sagwitch came to him and asked him to visit the Indian camp to explain why Brigham Young and a small party were on their way to visit the area. Pohnanteer met with twenty-five chiefs of the two tribes and it is quite possible that Pocatello was one of them. One of the chiefs asked, "What the hell does all this talk mean? . . . about Brigham Young coming here with Two Thousand men to use us up." When Pohnanteer explained that Young's party consisted of only thirteen vehicles and included nine women, the chief replied, "that did not look much like fighting." The Indian leaders then explained that the government officers at Fort Bridger had urged them "to fight and plunder the 'Mormons,'" and that apparently the Indians were being used as "tools" by the white officials to provoke a war with the Saints. The conference ended with expressions of gratitude from the chiefs for Mormon friendship and anger at the "barbarous" treatment they continued to receive from the government.[31]

In support of the fact that Mormon settlers were still feeding the Indians, the *Salt Lake Herald* of July 3, 1870, reported that Peter Maughan, in Cache County, was expecting a visit from the Bannock very soon and was borrowing flour to meet the expected demands for food. Pocatello and his group could very well have been along to get a share of the "free will offerings" from the Mormon farmers.

Dimick B. Huntington also tried to emphasize Mormon concern for the welfare of Utah's Indians by writing a special letter directly to the commissioner of Indian affairs in Washington. He reported that he was sending the letter at the request of the tribes of Utah. After noting that "I do love them . . . & they observe the mosayic Law mutch more strict to day than the whites do," Huntington tried to justify the various Indian attacks made over the years in Utah against whites because the natives had only acted according to their traditions and laws. He mentioned the massacre of the Capt. John W. Gunnison survey party on the Sevier River in

October 1853, the raids which had led to Colonel Connor's attack on the Shoshoni at Bear River, and then, "Pocatello the Shoshone Chief done what he done in retaliation for the killing of his sister by the whites." Except for this cryptic comment by the Mormon guide, we have no other information about this last incident which probably referred to the revenge taken by Pocatello at Massacre Rocks in 1862.[32]

The roaming Shoshoni of Utah and Idaho did have the option, by 1870, of settling upon the Fort Hall Reservation where Agent Danilson reported 520 occasional Bannock and 256 Shoshoni, mostly from the Boise and Bruneau bands.[33] In July, Tahgee and about three hundred Bannock and a hundred Shoshoni "from Bear River Valley, Utah" came into the reservation. They wanted the clothing ration promised under their treaty and a "big talk" with the Idaho superintendent of Indian affairs. Because the annuity goods had not arrived, Tahgee told the agent "unless something was done for them very soon he would not stand it." Danilson was saved by the timely arrival of $3,000 for the purchase of the clothing.[34]

The Shoshoni from Bear River may well have been Pocatello and some of his followers because a little later, DeLancey Floyd-Jones, Idaho superintendent of Indian affairs, reported a "big talk" or council held at Fort Hall with the Shoshoni there. Such Boise and Bruneau leaders as Captain Jim and Bruneau Jim explained that they had no horses, emphasized their desires to stay permanently at Fort Hall, and asked when blankets and other provisions would be given them. On the other hand, Pocatello responded with, "Me stop in Mormon house, me come to Fort Hall to see you—You talk, me go to Mormon house & tell Indians—All my Indians in Mormon house & in Buffalo Country—Me no want to stop here—Me stop on Deep Creek—My Agent at Box Center give me blanket clothing etc He gives me oxen, plow, powder etc." Captain Jim reinforced this accurate description of Pocatello's life-style at the time by saying, "I and my people want to remain here—Pocatello, he no stop here."[35] J. E. Tourtellotte of the Utah superintendency supported Pocatello's description, "They [Northwestern Shoshoni] have no permanent place of abode, but rove among the mountains and valleys wherever they find the best hunting and fishing. They cultivate

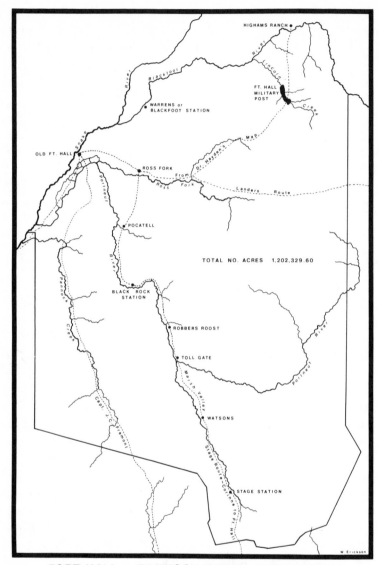

FORT HALL OR **BANNOCK INDIAN RESERVATION**
IDAHO, 1875

no land; . . . they must be moved from their present locality, as most of the arable land in this part of the Territory is already taken up by white citizens."[36] From this time on, there was increasing government pressure to get all the Northwestern bands, including Pocatello's, to move to Fort Hall.

True to his word about being near the Mormon settlements, Pocatello and other Northwestern chiefs assembled their bands at the camp near Corinne by mid-November 1870. The *Corinne Daily Utah Reporter* of November 11, 1870, described a variegated scene on the main street of the town as the citizens, some Chinese traders, and numerous Shoshoni gathered to see a demonstration of the new fire hydrants of the municipal waterworks. "Even old Pokatello who has avoided white settlements for two years past, honored (?) the occasion with his presence; as well as some fifty of his band who haven't stolen any white children in six months or so."

By November 16, Utah Governor Vernon H. Vaughan, Colonel Tourtellotte, and Agent Danilson had arrived "to disburse the quota of goods to Pokatello's band and other 'noble reds' who have been swarming around Corinne for some days."[37] Although nine other chiefs were there, again the local press highlighted the notorious Pocatello. The editor described how "ten thousand dollars worth of the people's property" was distributed to about three hundred Indians. The list of goods given out included one red shirt to each Indian, blankets, fishhooks, pans, pots, traps, hatchets, butcher knives, and combs to a "few of the copper colored maidens."[38] The editor was in error, however—only $5,000 worth of goods was distributed.[39]

After the fall distribution of goods, about three hundred Shoshoni continued to maintain their camp on Bear River just outside of Corinne throughout the next year, 1871, although it is probable that Pocatello and the mobile party of his band left to hunt buffalo again in Wyoming. Some of the Indians could be seen on the town's streets almost every day, and the *Corinne Reporter* ran frequent one liners about "ye gentle savage" and less flattering comments. The starving natives searched the garbage cans for food, caught rides on passing Central Pacific freight trains, enjoyed the local baseball games, bought liquor from unscrupulous white traders, did chores for the whites to earn a little money, gambled on the boardwalks, and were just too numerous "for the general good."[40]

More serious exchanges occurred between the Indians and citizens of the town. In one instance, a drunken Shoshoni man forced his way into a house, stole food, and broke up some of the furniture for a campfire. The city marshal had to drive him out.[41] In a second incident, another Indian entered a local judge's house and while engaged in stealing some "cutlery," was interrupted by the local magistrate, who grabbed a shovel and knocked the thief unconscious. His comrades outside rescued him and fled to the Bear River camp.[42] Members of Pocatello's band could have been involved in these affairs because a few of them were evidently part of the encampment.

The *Corinne Daily Journal* reported on June 16, 1871, that a "Grand Powwow" was underway on the banks of the Bear River, two miles from Corinne, involving a number of Shoshoni "lately returned from their annual buffalo hunt in the Wind River country." There were chiefs representing Shoshoni tribes from Utah, Nevada, Idaho, and Wyoming, and the grand council must surely have included Pocatello. The Indians seemed to be well supplied with greenbacks, and many patronized the local bank.[43]

About two weeks after the powwow, Agent M. P. Berry of the Fort Hall Reservation wrote the commissioner that a citizen on his way to Montana from Corinne "had been overtaken and surrounded by a band of Indians under the leadership of one Poc-a-tel-lah, a wandering Shoshone." The chief and his men "forcibly dispossessed" the man of his horse, recently purchased at Corinne, and were only prevented from killing the owner by the presence of other travelers en route to the mines. Berry continued, "This Poc-a-tel-lah and his band, some twelve in number, is I am further informed a species of outlaw and should be curbed before he proceeds to further outrages. I am further informed that he is a terror to the settlers wherever he goes—that he impudently levies upon them whenever he desires."[44]

Five days later, the *Corinne Journal* reported an attack on the Garrison & Wyatt freight train about twelve miles north of the town. The editor, however, thought that the story was a "huge joke" perpetrated by the local liverymen to profit from outfitting a relief party sent to the rescue of the freighters.[45] Pocatello's dangerous presence along the Montana Trail, however, carried little humor for small parties who could not adequately defend themselves.

Pocatello refused to starve like many of the other Northwestern Shoshoni and followed aggressive instincts to take what he needed from the whites who had possessed his country. As Agent Berry explained to the commissioner, he wished to settle the Shoshoni and Bannock permanently at Fort Hall to put an end to their "doubtful and precarious method of making a living by hunting Buffalo—of which there is none within Six hundred miles." But he would need a large appropriation to purchase enough flour and beef to feed the Indians once they were settled down.[46]

Pocatello and other chiefs knew there would not be enough to feed all the Indians congregated at the reservation. Many followed the example of the small band at Franklin in Cache Valley who were in a "helpless condition" and depended upon the Mormon residents of the town to feed them. Mayor L. H. Hatch wrote the Utah superintendent of Indian affairs that his citizens could no longer care for the "half starved Indians" who had been given food ever since Franklin's founding.[47] At Corinne and Ogden, Berry reported, the Indians lived "on the offal of Slaughter Houses and by acting as general scavengers for such places. The Mormon Bishop at Brigham City, occasionally issues from their private stores, Wheat or Flour, to such as live near that place."[48] The Corinnethians refused to participate in similar humanitarian policies and kept calling on public officials to stop the raids of Pocatello and others who refused to beg and just took what they needed.

Responding to their fears, Berry traveled to Corinne in late September 1871 to try to induce the Indians to return to the reservation. He found two lodges of "Pocatellahs people" and ordered them to leave for Fort Hall immediately, but refused to disturb about two hundred and fifty "souls, [who] were recognized as having ever been on this Reservation."[49] This may have been Sagwitch's band.

The year 1872 really belonged to a new special Indian agent for the Shoshoni of Utah, Dr. George W. Dodge, a verbose man of the

Fort Hall Agency Indians awaiting food on "Ration Day." *Utah State Historical Society.*

cloth whose heart usually ruled his head. He arrived in the territory in late December 1871 and began at once to search "for the whereabouts of my wards."[50] He soon learned that a portion of the Northwestern Shoshoni, very likely some of Pocatello's band, were being supplied by the agent at Fort Hall so he intended to withhold any of his supplies from them. Within a few weeks, also, he became convinced that the Mormon civil and ecclesiastical authorities "have been tampering with these Indians" and began a year's campaign to convince the Washington Office of Indian Affairs that strong action must be taken against the Saints.[51] In addition, he must have shocked the commissioner right out of his boots when he requested $125,000 to supply the Shoshoni for the year.[52] The Indians could certainly have benefited from that sum, which was many times larger than the actual appropriations for previous years.

Without authorization from the commissioner's office, Dr. Dodge dispersed food supplies quite liberally to the Shoshoni closest from his headquarters in Salt Lake City. The *Corinne Reporter* of February 2, 1872, described how under Dodge's orders about four hundred Northwestern Shoshoni near the town were given rations equal to four pounds of beef for each member of the encampment, a highly unusual and welcome report for Pocatello's and Sagwitch's people. The intolerant newspaper called it "Stuffing Savages." As soon as he learned of this largesse, the commissioner sent immediate orders to Dodge to stop the distribution and cancel all the supply contracts for provisions for the Indians in Utah. In an eight-page response, Dr. Dodge wrote, "It is the most painfull step I have ever been called upon to take. . . . How the Indians are to live without food, I know not. . . . If *they can,* they have different stomachs, . . . *generally* from mine." He continued that the Indian women often sold "themselves for a morsel of food. . . . What shall I do now? Say to these poor, sick, starving creatures, I can do no more?"[53]

By late April, Dodge accepted the realities of miniscule appropriations and was doing the best he could. He was more critical of the Northwestern bands than the Gosiute and Western Shoshoni and wrote of the Northwestern, "They roam here and there, through the northern part of this Territory, and give me more trouble by their incessant begging, gambling away, or selling of their goods,

than *all* others." Furthermore, he did not like the way they mingled
with the Mormons, and he especially singled out Dimick B. Huntington as a "bad man" who influenced them to mischief. He attempted to "vaxinate" the group near Corinne for smallpox and also
treated some of them for venereal disease. He even used $200 to
purchase tobacco for them because they *"will have it,* even at the
sacrifice of their clothing and other articles."[54] Pocatello and his
people would probably never again meet up with an Indian agent
such as Dr. Dodge.

Dodge's suspicions about the Mormons instigating Indians to
hostility against the government reached full bloom by July 1872.
In a twenty-four-page letter, filled with accusations and diatribe, he
outlined for the commissioner a supposedly monstrous plan con-
cocted by Brigham Young to foment an Indian war. Washakie and
his tribe, Indians from Fort Hall and Idaho, "including Po-ka-tel-lo
whom Gen Conner fought, and his band of Shoshones," all were
congregating in northern Utah in a *"mysterious movement."* There
were six thousand Sioux, Cheyenne, and other tribes at Camas Prairie in Idaho, "all heading this way," according to Dodge. The chiefs
had sent word that they would never surrender their lands, but that
they had given the Mormons permission to settle on the land. A
Paiute prophet from Walker River was stirring up the tribes. A
single word from Brigham Young would send all the Indians back to
their respective reservations, but the Mormon leader refused to give
it. The Mormons believed the Indians were descended from the Lost
Tribes of Israel and, therefore, intended to supervise the Indians
who were in rebellion against the government.[55] With such an im-
flammatory Indian agent at work, other Indian officials could only
hope that such restless chiefs as Pocatello would remain at peace.

The chairman of the board of Indian commissioners, Felix R.
Brunot, had an opportunity to test Pocatello's feelings about west-
ern affairs and the condition of the Indians at Fort Hall Reservation
on August 15, 1872, when he held a council there. Brunot and
Agent Johnson N. High met with the "head chief of the Fort Hall
Shoshones, Captain Jim," one of the Boise Shoshoni, and with
Pocatello, Sandy, Otter Beard, and Ty-ee, sub-chiefs. Already the
agent assigned Pocatello a lower status in favor of Captain Jim,

whose father, Peiem, had been one of the most prominent Shoshoni leaders from 1818 to 1828. Captain Jim was now a farmer and a very cooperative Indian leader at Fort Hall. He told Brunot in the meeting, "I am only a little chief. All the big chiefs are dead. . . . Tygee, the great Bannock chief, is dead." Perceptively, he also commented that who was or was not a great chief depended "upon what Washington says." Brunot asked, "If Captain Jim is chief over all, would Pocatello stay?" Captain Jim answered, "You can judge of that as well as I can." Captain Jim also informed the commissioner, "Pocatello has eleven lodges here, and some away hunting, but all will be in this fall." Then Brunot turned to Pocatello, "Would Pocatello like to remain here always?" The Northwestern leader answered, "Yes; but I would like sometimes to go off hunting." Brunot then had the following conversation with Pocatello:

> Mr. Brunot: Can Pocatello plow?
> Pocatello: I never tried it.
> Mr. Brunot: Pocatello ought to have a farm, and plow, and raise wheat and potatoes.
> Pocatello: We have nothing to work with. If we had tools we would work.
> Agent High: I have not helped Pocatello's band because they do not belong to me.
> Mr. Brunot: I will ask Washington to let Pocatello have a farm here for himself and his people.
> Pocatello: If we had a plow and horses, me and my people would stay here and work, but we have nothing to work with.
> Mr. Brunot: I will ask Washington where Pocatello is to stay, whether down by Corinne or here, and Washington will send word to Mr. High where he shall stay.[56]

But, as we shall see, word from Washington was long in coming. Eventually Pocatello concluded the matter by settling at Fort Hall—with or without the agent's or the government's approval.

After the Brunot council, Pocatello was thrown back to the reluctant support of Agent High at Fort Hall and the ineffective help of Reverend Dodge in Utah. The latter complained to the commissioner in August that six hundred of the Northwestern group were at Logan in Cache Valley begging for food and levying the settlers for subsistence, "claiming their due for rentage" of their land now occupied by the settlers. In the twenty-nine-page letter, Dodge concluded, "I am scarcely able physically to make this report," which leads a latter-day scholar to think that if he had written shorter letters and not so many of them he might have had more energy.[57]

An October 28, 1872, Dodge letter included a reputed excerpt from a Mormon council presided over by Brigham Young in which the church leader was supposed to have said, "We, as brothers, must do all in our power to get the Indians to commit all the depredations possible."[58] The commissioner finally tired of Dodge's constant complaints and obvious ineffectiveness and sent word that his special agency was being discontinued "on account of a supposed excess of instructions in my official administration," as Dodge so well expressed his failure.[59] Pocatello and other Northwestern Shoshoni were left to deal with Agent Johnson High at Fort Hall.

On December 5, 1872, High reported to the commissioner that after receiving their annuities from Dodge at Corinne, Pocatello and three hundred of his people had shown up at the reservation intending to winter there and make it their home. High wrote:

> There seems to be no chief of real consequence among them. Pocatella says he is no chief, but that his brother [probably Pocatello Tom] and a man named John [Pocatello John, a member of the band but no relation to Chief Pocatello] and one whose name I don't know and who stops near Ogden, Utah, are the chiefs. While these men are chiefs, Pocatello is really the business man among them and is so recognized by being virtually head chief. A few years ago he got into trouble and was arrested by the military officials once or twice and has learned that there is a disability as well as honors connected with the chieftainship. Hence while he performs the duties he declines the honor.

Pocatello's actions are quite understandable. Agents or other white officials usually chose as reservation chiefs individuals who would "go along" so they could "get along" and were amenable to the suggestions provided them by the whites in charge. So, when Pocatello was approached as an obvious candidate to represent his band as chief, he declined. Acceptance would have placed him in the odious position of being blamed for most of the inescapable troubles which reservation life ensured. He no doubt wanted to remain a trusted Shoshoni leader and refused to accept what to him was an offensive offer to become a reservation chief.[60]

High wanted Pocatello to lead his band back to the Corinne area where the Utah officials should take care of them. But the resident Indians at Fort Hall insisted that Pocatello be allowed to stay, and they agreed to share their provisions with his people. The agent proposed Pocatello's people be allowed to stay permanently at the reservation instead of being "scattered along the Rail Road and Among the Mormon settlements." He, of course, expected a proper appropriation so he could subsist them.[61]

But sufficient funds never came as more and more Shoshoni decided to make their homes at Fort Hall. The town of Corinne, therefore, suffered from the lack of subsistence at the reservation as the Indians continued to camp on the Bear River and alternated between begging for food at nearby Brigham City and just hanging around Corinne. The Shoshoni women gleaned the wheat fields in the area and the men stole rides on the railroad freight cars and loitered "about the city, drunk or sober, at all hours," according to the *Corinne Reporter* of February 21, 1872. There were incidents of violence as drunken Indians broke into houses and local hotels or tried shoplifting at the stores. When news came of the murder of some army officers by the Modoc Indians in California, the indignant Corinne newspaper editor noted that the Shoshoni had decided to hold a war dance outside of town "in honor of the Modoc victory. They ought to be skinned alive for their insolence."[62] Some of Pocatello's people and the chief himself were very likely occasional visitors at the rather permanent Bear River Indian encampment.

Thus, the years from 1865 through 1972 marked significant changes in Pocatello's relationship with the government. The occasional efforts by Indian officials to feed and clothe the no longer self-sufficient Northwestern bands were highlighted by the annual distribution of presents on lower Bear River. The various agents made occasional halfhearted attempts to give the Indians cattle to get them started as stock raisers but usually discovered that the natives had eaten the stock to offset starving. The Mormons were still feeding Pocatello and his fellow chiefs and their bands, although the burden was leading the Saints more and more to complain and to ask the government to relieve them of the necessity.

Perhaps the most interesting development during this period was the changing perception that Fort Hall officials came to have of Pocatello, mainly because he decreed it. When Johnson High attempted to deal with the Indian leader as the chief of his band, Pocatello refused to accept the "honor" although High recognized that he was the commanding leader. Pocatello had no difficulty in establishing his authority over his people away from the reservation but refused to become a bureaucratic chief or to deal with agency officials. He preferred to let Pocatello John or his two brothers, Pocatello Tom and Pocatello Pete, deal with reservation problems. From this time on, and especially when he settled permanently at Fort Hall after 1875, Pocatello's name appears only infrequently in agency records and reports. Pocatello John and Pocatello's two brothers took over the management of affairs. Pocatello found it difficult to give up his roaming and agree to a new kind of life with white men he did not trust. It would take only another three years, however, before he would have to accept the reservation as his final home.

6

A Starving Time and a
Religious Experience

For twenty-five years, from the arrival of the Mormon settlers in 1847 to 1873, Pocatello and the other Northwestern Shoshoni chiefs and their people had watched with ever-increasing despair and hunger as white farmers plowed the land and appropriated the springs that had provided game and grass seeds for Indian subsistence. As food conditions became more and more desperate, they and their concerned Indian agents attempted to persuade an indifferent government that a permanent home should be located for them in their own territory. That was no longer possible by the 1870s, so some officials began to sponsor a movement to place all the Northwestern bands as well as those in Idaho on the newly founded Fort Hall Reservation. The Indians were interested in the reserve as the last possibility for a home, but early visits to Fort Hall soon alerted them that there was not enough food to support all the Indians congregating there. Many, therefore, as did Pocatello, went on trips to the Plains to hunt buffalo, met their agents at the lower Bear River to accept niggardly amounts of "presents," and haunted Mormon farmsteads looking for food. Whites and Shoshoni alike were looking for a solution to the problem of sustaining the wandering bands.

Eventually, the government established a commission, in 1873, under J. W. Powell and G. W. Ingalls to examine the condition of the Utes, Paiutes, Gosiutes, Western Shoshoni, and the Northwestern Shoshoni "for the purpose of consulting with them concerning the propriety of their removal to reservations." The commissioners traveled to Curlew Valley, Cache Valley, and Deep Creek to meet with the Northwestern and Gosiute chiefs and held a council with a number of them and other Indian leaders as well at Salt Lake City.[1] During the long process of traveling around and trying to meet with the diverse groups, Commissioner Ingalls wired Washington, D.C., on June 13, 1873, "Just returned met Sanpits & Tabanshea who agree to see Seigwits and Pocatilla—all object to fort Hall but will go with Nevada shoshone & on a reservation seventy five miles south west fort Hall fine country few settlers can both be united one agency."[2]

This was, of course, in the Raft River and Grouse Creek area and may have indicated Pocatello's attempt to influence Ingalls's perception of a possible reservation site. But five days later, Powell recommended to the commissioner in Washington that the Northwestern bands should meet him and Ingalls at Fort Hall, that future annuities would only be distributed to the Northwestern Shoshoni at that place, and that "the Fort Hall reservation is to be their future home."[3] The commissioner approved the recommendations and ordered Powell and Ingalls to proceed with their plans.[4]

Powell's intentions were noble, but he did not reckon with the uncertain movements of the Northwestern bands, whom he finally had to meet at the usual place on the Bear River for the distribution of annuities for 1873. The *Deseret News* of November 10, 1873, printed a long article concerning the commissioner's work and the annuity meeting. The reporter indicated that three hundred Indians had assembled at the Bear River under "San Pits" and "Swiquits" and that "There is another tribe, greater in numbers, on the Fort Hall reservation," Pocatello's people. Powell and Ingalls supervised the distribution of goods, which the reporter listed in great detail. He then wrote, "Steps are being taken to place the N.W. Shoshones on a reservation in Nevada. The Indians are willing and the matter will doubtless soon be accomplished."[5] The commissioner in Washington explained in his final report of the Powell-Ingalls Commission that they were unable to meet the Northwestern bands at Fort Hall and "It was found that a part of them, under a chief named Po-ka-tel-lo, had already gone to Fort Hall, and had signified their intention of remaining and taking part with the Shoshonies and Bannocks on that reservation."[6]

Powell later made a statement before the House Committee on Indian Affairs, on January 13, 1874, in which he noted that he and Ingalls had visited Fort Hall with Gen. John P. C. Shanks, who was there with a second commission to arrange a new agreement with the Fort Hall Indians. At the time, there were four hundred North-western Shoshoni among the 1,437 resident Indians on the reservation.[7] This was Pocatello's group.

General Shanks, along with Governor T. W. Bennett of Idaho Territory and Agent Henry W. Reed of Fort Hall, was appointed to negotiate an agreement concerned with trespass and other problems at Fort Hall and to obtain a "relinquishment" of the fourth article of the Treaty of Fort Bridger of July 3, 1868, "to hunt on any unoccupied land" of the United States. The commission met with the principal chiefs and Indians on November 7, 1873, and produced an agreement of eight articles which involved relinquishing the right to hunt on the unoccupied lands as well as a number of miscellaneous matters concerned with public roads, cattle trespass, and the boundaries of the reservation. The commission noted the lack of a chief with the "capacity to control and direct the several bands of Indians there" and recommended that Chief Tendoy of the Lemhi Shoshoni, "one of the noblest Indians in America," be moved from the Salmon River to Fort Hall to preside over affairs on the reservation. Ten major chiefs signed the agreement. "Bocatellah" was fifth in line and Pocatellah John sixth, after Captain Jim, Shoshoni chief, and Otter Beard, Pagwite, and Tyee, Bannock chiefs.[8]

The Boise Shoshoni leader, Captain Jim, was apparently the nominal head chief through whom the agent handled most reservation business, and Pocatello John also seemed to be rising in importance. The latter would soon come to represent the band led by Pocatello as that leader either refused to participate in reservation affairs or was deliberately overlooked by succeeding agents. Of course, it was also true that Chief Pocatello found it difficult to settle down to the prosaic business of farming. Old hunting pursuits and free movement were so enticing that he may not have been home on Bannock Creek long enough to get very involved in the early life of the reservation, especially when there was not enough food to go around. He was still too impatient to wait for rations that never showed up and would leave for the old haunts to search for subsistence or would just appropriate white property when there was no other way.

To complicate matters further, the desperate Indians at Fort Hall complained, in letters to Idaho Governor T. W. Bennett and to the commissioner of Indian affairs, that their agent, Henry W. Reed, was stealing their rations and selling the annuity goods for his own profit. To the governor, the Indians wrote:

> The President is our great father, but he is a great way off; we cannot speak loud enough for him to hear. . . . Our Agent does not care for us, but we are not mad. . . . Our women and children are hungry for flour and meat. For three weeks our children have been crying for food; in that time he has given us nothing. There is flour—hundreds of sacks—and beef cattle at the Agency. Why should we suffer? . . . While this Agent is here the chiefs cannot keep their people together at home. They go everywhere, and we are afraid will kill white people, as they did a few years ago. . . . He sells lumber, hogs, hay and beef hides. What does he do with the money? . . . Lots of Indians who have been here will not come back. . . . We want an Agent who always speaks the truth; who will not let us suffer.[9]

Among those who left the reservation during this period were Pocatello and most of his band. The letter to Bennett was signed by Captain Jim, Chief; Gibson Jack, Headman; Pocatello John, Chief; Jack Ballard, Headman; and Cash Valley Tom, Headman. Pocatello John was now speaking for those of Chief Pocatello's band who remained on the reservation.

The letter to the commissioner was a recitation of the same charges against Agent Reed but was signed by a different set of chiefs and headmen—Pagwite, Bannock Chief, and three lesser headmen. Pagwite complained that "Our young men are wild and we want to keep them where we can see them all the time. They are scattered, and we hardly know where to find them now." He added that "Some that we left here have gone to the Buffalo country and we are afraid they will be killed by the Sioux Indians." Very likely, Pocatello and his young warriors were a part of this group and spent the fall and winter of 1874–75 in Wyoming hunting buffalo and dodging Sioux war parties.[10]

Henry Reed was soon replaced at Fort Hall by James Wright, who continued the drumbeat of requests from the rapidly changing agents for more funds with which to buy food for the Indians. Wright warned the commissioner in a November 21, 1874, letter that unless sufficient beef was purchased to feed the Indians, "They will be compelled to rove and live as they can by stealing or begging."[11] The agent continued his appeals for help in a year-end letter indicating that the Shoshoni and Bannock desperately wanted to remain on the reservation, "but cannot do so unless they have something to eat."[12] Pocatello would not put up with such conditions, and, along with the similarly independent Bannock, refused to stay any longer at Fort Hall.

Then, by late 1874, a new hope for the Northwestern and other Shoshoni groups appeared when the Mormons decided upon a concerted effort to proselyte the Indians in northern Utah by establishing farms for them. In April 1874, Brigham Young had designated George W. Hill, a night watchman for the Union Pacific Railroad at Ogden, Utah, and already a part-time missionary among the Shoshoni at Lower Bear River, to head a full-time mission among the "Lamanites" of the area. On May 1, Hill baptized 101 Indians from the Northwestern Shoshoni band camped near Corinne and then moved to Franklin, Idaho, to work with another group who had been depending on the Mormon settlers for subsistence. He established an Indian farm near Franklin but after months of fruitless effort because of its poor location was forced to abandon the project and by early 1875 was back at Corinne.[13] Dimick B. Huntington was also involved in the missionary work at Franklin, and by August 9, 1874, the Mormon newspaper, the *Salt Lake Herald,* could proudly report that "there are some six hundred of the red men who are Latter-day Saints," many of them Shoshoni.

Back in the Brigham City area by December 1874, and at the request of the Pocatello and Sagwitch bands of the Northwestern Shoshoni and, of course, to help further his own missionary efforts, George Hill wrote the commissioner of Indian affairs explaining the predicament of the natives. He indicated to Washington that the

Missionaries baptizing Paiute Indians. In 1874 George W. Hill and Dimick B. Huntington baptized hundreds of Northwestern Shoshoni in northern Utah and southern Idaho into the Mormon Church. *Utah State Historical Society.*

Indians were "a continual expence" to him and asked why the $5,000 worth of annuity goods guaranteed the Indians each year under the Treaty of Box Elder had not been delivered for the two years past. Hill concluded that "they are in a suffering condition" and asked for immediate help for them from the government.[14] The Indian Office apparently pigeonholed the request.

But the evident poverty and suffering of the Shoshoni around Corinne led to ever-increasing and strident demands on the part of the Corinnethians that the government do something to relieve the annoyance caused by the Indians loitering around the town. The *Corinne Daily Mail* ran numerous editorials asking that whites who sold liquor to the Indians be prosecuted before Corinne "become[s] notorious for drunken Indians."[15] The paper noted that the Shoshoni appeared on the streets clad only in plug hats and moccasins and unless the Utah Indian agents furnished them more blankets, they would be "in danger of being snatched by the City Marshal for exposure of person."[16] While the citizens of Corinne ignored Shoshoni wants and attacked the government for not providing for them, Mormon Bishop Alvin Nichols of Brigham City distributed beef and other foods to the Indians, including very probably Pocatello's band, "on a liberal scale" in early November 1874.[17]

The Corinne newspapers, ever since the founding of the town in the spring of 1869, had attacked and ridiculed the Shoshoni who camped on the Bear River near the settlement and especially had shown concern for Mormon friendliness towards the natives. Adopting the attitude of many non-Mormons, the journals maintained that the Saints were instigating the local natives to oppose the government and to harass the gentile population. Fear that the Mormons were conspiring with the Shoshoni to overwhelm and destroy Corinne began to surface, at least on the part of the editor of the *Corinne Daily Mail,* in an article appearing December 7, 1874:

> A party of some two hundred Indians have spread their tents near Brigham City, and more are coming in daily. They say about nine hundred declare they will not stay on the reservation and in a short time will be in their camp. That they have been invited to come here by the citizens of Brigham City, and in case of any difficulty between the Gentiles and the Mormons they are to take the side of the Mormons. Their chief claims to be a Mormon bishop. No depredations have as yet been committed but the grand mogul has a war spear raised over his tent and says he intends to "hold his position."

In almost daily articles, the editor hammered away at this theme, noting that Indians were coming in great numbers from the Fort Hall Reservation determined to stay in the Corinne vicinity "until the government furnished blankets and supplies." Further-

Pokotel Tom. *Bureau of American Ethnology.*

Pokotel Pete. *Bureau of American Ethnology.*

Pocatello John (not the original Pocatello) and Major Pete Gallagher. *Idaho State Historical Society.*

more, the Indians were burning fences and stealing everything they could find unguarded. [18] The stage was being set for a real confrontation involving Chief Pocatello, Chief Sagwitch, and other Shoshoni leaders.

Pocatello's band and the other Indians at Fort Hall were faced with a hard choice in early 1875. They could remain on the reservation where Agent Wright wrote, "What these people will do I cannot tell." [19] On the other hand, they could leave the starving conditions at Fort Hall and move to the Corinne area where Mormon missionary George Hill offered opportunities to farm and to provide for their own subsistence. In such event, however, they would run the risk of serious trouble with antagonistic whites at Corinne or perhaps a battle with the military. [20] After proselyting at Franklin, Hill was given a special assignment by his church in April 1875 to establish a "Lamanite" mission farm near the Bear River, about seven miles north of Corinne. With the help of some of his recent Indian converts, he planted one hundred acres of wheat, twenty-five acres of corn, five and one-half of potatoes, and about six acres of garden vegetables, "the Indians taking hold of their work well." [21]

As Hill and his new Latter-day Saints began to construct a canal, to plan for houses, and to observe their new religion by participating in morning and evening prayers and by saying grace before meals, news of these wonderful doings began to circulate among Shoshoni groups at Wind River in Wyoming and at Salmon River among the Lemhi as well as Fort Hall. The Shoshoni recognized at once that membership in the Church of Jesus Christ of Latter-day Saints (LDS) Church could bring earthly rewards with immersion in a nearby stream being the minimum action in assuring food and sustenance. Soon, several hundred Indians had gathered at the farm, hoping to reap the benefits of learning to farm and to provide for themselves under Mormon tutelage. To Hill and his missionary associates, it was a wonderful opportunity to convert the Indians to Mormonism. They lost no time in holding baptismal services for the natives, who by this time were claiming the new farm for a reservation. [22]

Chief Pocatello, impulsive as ever, inaugurated the evangelistic proceedings by traveling to Salt Lake City to demand baptism. The *Deseret News* of May 5, 1875 reported:

More Lamanites Baptized.—On Tuesday night, Poko-tel-lo, a chief from the Snake River country, accompanied by his band, arrived in this city for the purpose of being baptized into the Church. The ceremony was attended to yesterday afternoon. Elder D. B. Huntington officiating, and they left for the north again soon after, feeling well, and satisfied with what they had heard, and determined to refrain from evil practices. Poko-tel-lo stated that there were many other Indians who intended to be baptized.

The *Deseret News* was in error about "D. B. Huntington officiating." Church records indicate that Elder Hyrum Mikesell baptized the new members, including in addition to Pocatello five Shoshoni men: Wong-go-cho, Pad-sey-to-by, Tis-si-merri-kip, Pah-yan-e-up, and To-se-pah-va-way; and four women: An-ne-sar-e-gip, Mo-to-so-rup, Ac-a-mo, and Pan-sack-goot-say. Elder John Cottam blessed two of the Indian children: Nah-wan-k-keep and Tabby-sho-gain. Cottam as "mouth" and assisted by Mikesell then ordained Pocatello an elder in the LDS Church.[23]

The chief was a true prophet in predicting other Indian baptisms. Hill was soon engulfed by continuing waves of eager converts seeking spiritual as well as physical salvation. On June 7, 1875, he baptized 168 Indians in nearby Bear River, and the process continued through August 1, when he immersed 292 individuals that one day, for a total of 574 new Saints for his summer's work.[24] Some of the converts were quite overcome by the emotional experience of being baptized. Hill recorded:

> There was also a singular thing transpired that Day [August 1] out of three hundred that were baptized that Day there were seven or eight all stout hearty people some men and some women that after I had raised them out of the water would wilt and become Lifeless in my arms . . . the Cheifs [*sic*] standing on the bank keeping count and telling me to give them time to come to and not hurry them.[25]

The migration of Indians from Wind River, Lemhi, and Fort Hall to the Mormon mission caused deep consternation among the agents who were trying to procure sufficient funds for food and otherwise stabilize their volatile charges. Fort Hall agent James Wright warned the commissioner on June 10 that a visit to Corinne and the Mormon Indian farm had convinced him that the several hundred

Indians he found there were "being operated upon by Mormons, many of them Baptized, others taken through the 'Endowment House' (whatever this is or means) and called 'The Lords Battle Axes.' . . . All this means mischief."[26] Dimick Huntington explained the process of granting endowments to the Shoshoni as he instructed Hill:

SL City August 6 [1875]
Brother G W Hill   Sir   Two weeks from today you may send down an other company of worthy men & women to go through. [Endowment House] & be sure to send a true list or make out to send their genealigy so that there will be no mistake. Send Jim with them let Jane come too. I went through to day all is well. Love to all.
D. B. Huntington
P S   Dont send more than 30 at once, on account of cloathing send them Monday evening to go through on Tuesday[27]

Three weeks after his June 10 letter, Agent Wright reemphasized his concern that it was impossible for him to keep the Indians from leaving Fort Hall for Hill's mission station at Bear River. "They go away in the night, and when they return deny that they have been there, and when pressed get mad. The Mormons have sent Indians to this Agency and Wind River to enlist the Indians in their favor." He predicted trouble unless the Indians were at once taken out of Utah.[28]

When William H. Danilson replaced James Wright in late July 1875 for a second stint as agent at Fort Hall, he reinforced the latter's warnings to the commissioner, reporting that Indian converts to Mormonism had been proselyting all summer among the reservation group at Fort Hall and that "large numbers have gone and are still going to Utah to get washed & greased and enrolling themselves in the cause of the Mormons. They are told they and the Mormons are the chosen ones of the Lord to establish his Kingdom on earth. They are taught to hate the government, and look with distrust upon their Agents."[29] In a later report, Danilson expounded further on supposed Mormon machinations among the natives who "were told that by being baptized and joining the Church the old men would never be sick, that the Lord had a work for them to do and that they were the chosen people of God to establish his Kingdom upon the earth etc etc   Also that Bear River Valley belonged to them and if the soldiers attempted to drive them away not to go as their guns would have no effect upon them. Their whole teachings were fraught with evil."[30]

If the agents at Fort Hall had misgivings about Mormon-Indian interaction at the mission farm, they could not match the excited hyperbole engendered by the editor of the *Corinne Daily Mail,* who, throughout the first six months of 1875, could spot a skulking Indian warrior behind every bush with a malevolent Mormon elder conveniently nearby, both ready to pounce upon the defenseless citizens of gentile Corinne. In such an inflammatory climate, it was not long before the *Corinne Daily Mail* initiated what became known as the "Corinne Indian Scare," an event in which Pocatello played a prominent role.[31]

The scare the *Mail* ignited finally resulted in the expulsion of the Indians from the Mormon farm and their forced withdrawal back to their respective reservations. This came on the heels of the trial of John D. Lee at Beaver, Utah, on charges that he had led a united force of Indians and Mormons in the infamous Mountain Meadows Massacre of 1857. On August 7, 1875, the jury in the trial was discharged when it could not reach a verdict, and the *Corinne Daily Mail* seized upon the mistrial as proof that the Mormons and their Indian allies would now be free to perpetrate other murders.[32]

With such scare headlines as "Mormons Meddling with Indians! Mountain Meadows to be Repeated!," the residents of Corinne became so distraught and afraid that they finally succumbed to a "Night of Terror!" inspired by the jingoistic newspaper editor. The story can be summarized. According to the *Mail,* a horde of savage warriors was advancing on the town. Women and children were placed in local hotels or sent to Ogden for safety; armed men went out into the night to repel the Indian invaders; and Mayor E. P. Johnson wired Governor George W. Emery for troops to be sent posthaste from Fort Douglas in Salt Lake City. When a company of fifty soldiers arrived the next day, their commander, Capt. James Kennington, together with Mayor Johnson and an interpreter, went to the Indian camp and found that there was "no more danger than there is of an attack on the people of New York." Nevertheless, the captain issued an ultimatum that all reservation Indians were to return to their reservations at once or he would use military force to compel them to do so. George Hill protested but to no avail. Two other companies of troops arrived the next day, August 12, to reinforce Kennington's order, and Pocatello and other Fort Hall and Wind River Indians hurriedly took down their tipis and left. Behind them, they abandoned fields ready for the harvest—an entire year's effort at farming. It was a hard blow for the Indians and a major defeat for Mormon Indian policy, although the prevailing mood of the time inevitably assured that the Shoshoni would be concentrated on reservations.

In the conference with the military commander and Mayor Johnson, the *Salt Lake Tribune* reporter wrote that "the Indians, through their chiefs, Pocatella, Little Soldier, and one whose name I could not catch but hailing from Fort Hall, said they wanted to be friends with all the whites; that they had been gathered there by representations made them by the Mormons, that they were wanted to occupy the land in that valley, which they (Mormons) said they owned."[33] Sagwitch probably spoke for all the chiefs when he turned to George Hill and said, "Don't talk to me—you have lied to me and my heart is sick." And to Captain Kennington, he said, "What have I stolen? Who have I killed? What meanness have I done?"[34]

From the point of view of Agent Danilson at Fort Hall, the "Corinne Indian Scare" and the arrival of the Camp Douglas troops was a good thing. He reported that the frightened Shoshoni were flocking to the reservation for protection including 120 converts who had left Fort Hall for the Bear River farm. Most of these were probably from Pocatello's band. Danilson wrote the commissioner that "They had no idea of fighting the troops, and when ordered by them to leave started at once. They seem very much disgusted with the whole proceeding. Some lost faith in the Mormons, and say they did not know they were doing anything in opposition to the Government."[35] Except for about three hundred of the Mormon converts who later settled in Malad Valley at a place called Washakie under church auspices, the balance of the over six hundred initial neophyte Indians, including Chief Pocatello, probably became apostates from their faith, and some of their descendants at Fort Hall retain a bitterness to this day toward the LDS Church.[36]

As an aftermath of the Corinne scare, Chief Pocatello was credited, at least by the Corinne newspaper, with planning a concerted attack on Mormon settlers in Cache Valley. The Mormon *Salt Lake Herald* of August 17, 1875, poked fun at the very idea and quoted the *Corinne Daily Mail:*

> Reports received here to-day state the Indians recently expelled from this valley for an attempted raid upon Corinne have not returned to their reservations, as ordered by government officers. Reliable parties returning from the Cache Valley, say Pocatello, with his entire band and several smaller companies of Indians, are encamped near Logan, about 20 miles from here. They are at least 1,500 in number, and are being supported entirely by Mormons, and under control of the Mormon church. Considerable apprehension is felt by the people of this city that *another attack* will be made. The citizens have been furnished with needle guns and other arms belonging to the government, and pickets are stationed around the city every night.

It is quite possible that Pocatello was at Logan. His refusal to follow military orders would be in keeping with his risk-taking and resolute character. He was still used as an ogre to frighten timid civilians when by this time he wanted only a peaceful home and food for his people.

In another edition, the editor of the *Mail* used an incident about Pocatello as a means of fueling the Corinnethian's ridicule of Mormon practices. The story represented, also, the widespread white impressions of Pocatello as an Indian leader of audacity and rough humor:

> *Pocatello and the Garments.*—Pocatello, the chief of several hundred Indians, who were removed from this neighborhood last week, when going north met a gentleman and inquired of him if he was a Mormon. Receiving a reply that he was, Pocatello remarked "Me good Mormon too," and insisted upon examining him to see if he wore the endowment robes—the garments. To satisfy him he consented, and exhibited them. The chief was very much pleased, and spying the Mormon's wife wished to know if "she good Mormon," also. "Oh, yes; she's my wife," was the answer. The dusky rascal, however, looked dubious, and saying: "Heap dam, no believe; me see," started towards the wagon to test the matter of the endowment robes, and only by super-

human efforts in smothering his laughter, and with the best of talk did the husband convince and induce him to forego his intention.[37]

Aware of the freewheeling and rather loose editorial policies of the *Corinne Daily Mail,* this tale might well be apocryphal, a deliberate bit of fiction devised to satisfy the editor's penchant for lambasting the Mormons. If so, the selection of Pocatello as the main character does illustrate his current notoriety. On the other hand, knowing Pocatello's reputation for boldness in dealing with whites and his recent disillusionment with the Mormons, the story might very well be true.

The years from 1873 through 1875 were pivotal for Pocatello and other Northwestern Shoshoni leaders. Deprived of the opportunity to gain any help from George Hill's operations at Bear River, the disconsolate ex-Mormon chief led his people back to Fort Hall, where they faced a continued shortage of food supplies and no help in learning how to farm. To a free-roaming chieftain, the prospect of confinement to a reservation and the bureaucratic political infighting which seemed to be normal there, was disheartening indeed. As we shall see, he just withdrew from any active participation in reservation affairs, never becoming a contented resident of Fort Hall.

7

Last Years at Fort Hall

After his return to the Fort Hall Reservation by the winter of 1876, the once-prominent Pocatello seemed to drop from sight. The newspapers of northern Utah that had followed his career with some interest and apprehension for years give no account of him after the "Corinne Indian Scare." Similarly, and because of his inclination to stay out of reservation affairs, Fort Hall and government records mention him only occasionally. Only assumptions can be made about what his life was like during his last years, noting that he did not participate in important events or movements at the Fort Hall Reservation.

Agent Danilson informed the Indian commissioner in February 1876 that whereas only five Indian families had cultivated farms of their own during the preceding summer, now another twenty families had agreed to commence farming if furnished with sufficient implements. The new would-be farmers had selected a site on Bannock Creek, about thirty miles from the agency, to begin life as agriculturists. As Danilson wrote, "They have good soil, plenty of water & timber for irrigating and building purposes."[1] Pocatello and some of his people had always looked upon Bannock Creek as part of their homeland. When Pocatello and his band settled there, they disappeared from reservation history, because the Bannock Creek settlement was twenty-five miles away from the central agency and so isolated that from then until now the Indian families living there have been somewhat neglected by the agents and have not played an important part in the history of Fort Hall.

Pocatello was bothered by the crowding of the Boise Shoshoni at Fort Hall but was even more concerned that his people get away from all other bands so they could retain their identity and independence. His people and the Fort Hall Shoshoni and Bannock did not get along well. They were comfortable camping with Cache Valley Shoshoni, with other Northwestern groups, or with Washakie, but they wanted isolation from other Shoshoni. They would not allow Bannock people in their country at all. Furthermore, they avoided mixing with the Bannock at Fort Hall. Other Shoshoni sent to Fort Hall did not get along with the bands already at the reservation, and there is still factionalism resulting from these pre-1869 conflicts. White government officials should have anticipated that consolidating bands from different areas and of different and independent ways on one small reserve would cause problems. Even if some Indian officials had such transitory thoughts, they easily dismissed them. The Shoshoni had no choice in the matter.

Any Shoshoni with sufficient initiative and industry to strike out on their own as farmers were quite evidently following the only course to survival, as Danilson's constant reports indicated. On April 20, 1876, he informed Washington that "About one thousand Indians have been thrown upon their own resources and are obliged to get their living as best they can. . . . They come to the office with tears in their eyes begging most piteously for food for their children to eat. Would to God that those who hold the destiny of these people in their hands could be here to see for themselves, their necessities."[2]

To add to the starvation threat, rumors began circulating at Fort Hall that the government intended to send troops to drive the Shoshoni and Bannock to the Oklahoma Indian Territory. In desperation, six of the reservation headmen traveled to Boise in July 1876 to appeal to the governor of Idaho Territory to stop the military action and to lay other troubles before him. The Indian leaders were listed as Captain Jim, Gibson Jack, Pagwite, Tetowaba, Captain Jack, and Major George.[3] Chief Pocatello was not a delegation member.

The following year was marked by the Nez Perce War and the flight of many of the tribe under Chief Joseph and other leaders into Montana Territory, a conflict having repercussions for the Indians at

Fort Hall. Starving conditions there forced most of the Indians to leave and by June 1877 about fifteen hundred Fort Hall Shoshoni, Bannock, and Lemhi Shoshoni were gathered at Camas Prairie in central Idaho to harvest camas roots for winter food. When news came to Boise that the Nez Perce warriors were attempting to enlist Shoshoni in the conflict with the U.S. troops, Boise Mayor Thomas E. Logan and I. N. Coston traveled to Camas Prairie to confer with the fourteen chiefs assembled there, each chief claiming equal authority. The two officials arranged to have five of the principal leaders travel to Boise to meet with Governor Mason Brayman. The five chiefs listed were Captain Jim of the Boise Shoshoni, Major Jim representing the Bannock, Tetoka who was filling in for Tendoy of the Lemhi, Major George for the Bannock, and Bannock John from Salmon Falls.[4] Again, Pocatello was not at the meeting. He could very well have been one of the fourteen chiefs mentioned; gathering camas roots was an important food activity for all the Indians at Fort Hall.

The following month, Capt. Augustus H. Bainbridge, in command of the military post at Fort Hall, visited the Indian agency to ensure that the Shoshoni and Bannock did not get embroiled in the Nez Perce War. He talked with "Tagher [Tyhee] and Pagwite (who are the principal Bannock and Shoshoni Chiefs at that Agency), and many other representative Indians."[5] Again, no mention of Pocatello. He was either absent from the reservation or determined not to get involved in such conferences.

Agent Danilson gave Captain Bainbridge a report on the whereabouts of his charges as of June 21, 1877. There were 510 Indians engaged in farming, and 100 "coming and going," for a total of 610 on the reservation. About 700 were at Camas Prairie and the Goose Creek Mountains, 50 hanging around the settlements in Cache Valley, and 150 in the mountains between Fort Hall and Virginia City, Montana.[6] Pocatello could have been gravitating between farming on Bannock Creek or, more likely, hunting in the Goose Creek Mountains, his old homeland.

A settler living near Bear Lake, W. P. Nebeker, reported during February 1878 about hostile Shoshoni and Bannock activity during the previous summer, a reaction no doubt to the Nez Perce War. Nebeker thought an outright war had been averted only by the patience and forbearance of the settlers under great provocation from the Indians. The natives had turned their ponies into the fields and broken down fences, saying "contemptuously . . . that the land belonged to them." They were "very harsh, in many instances, in their treatment of the families of the settlers, entering houses in an austere or violent manner and demanding bread etc. which if not forthcoming on the instant . . . was in most cases followed by heavy blows of sticks or riding whips administered to females and children." Nebeker asked that the Indians be kept on their reservations or, if allowed to visit the settlements, that the Office of Indian Affairs control "their abusive and violent conduct." He was certain that Chief Joseph's war with U.S. troops had inflamed the Shoshoni and Bannock, who approved the Nez Perce attacks on the army and who "felt full of fight themselves, and that a very slight indiscretion on the part of a settler was likely to precipitate a conflict."[7] As in other instances of this kind, one can only speculate whether Pocatello and his band were involved. Such an opportunity would have been hard to resist. Very likely, some Bannock were implicated. Some of them were already attuned to the desirability of making war on settlers who were destroying their food supplies.

The outbreak of the Bannock War in the summer of 1878 offered Pocatello and like-minded aggressive chiefs another opportunity to cause trouble. The restive Bannock, angered by the government's broken promises to provide food at Fort Hall while they learned to farm and excited by the Nez Perce outbreak, had shown signs of rebellion in the fall of 1877, which culminated in the shooting of two white teamsters by a Bannock named Tambiago. After a very tense winter at the reservation, in late May, about two hundred Bannock warriors under Buffalo Horn started hostilities after objecting to the destruction of camas roots at Camas Prairie by the hogs and cattle of white owners. The Bannock War ended after a summer of fox-and-hounds chase in Oregon, Idaho, and Montana.[8]

The record does not indicate what Pocatello's attitude was. Col. John O. Smith, who was sent from Camp Douglas to control the rebellious Bannock at Fort Hall, reported in December 1877 that he had had "an interview with the Head Men of the Bannocks and Shoshones, neither band having any chief."[9] Pocatello was evidently not important enough or visible enough to attract any military attention. It is noteworthy that a reporter for the *Idaho Statesman*, writing of his investigation of affairs at Fort Hall on March 2, 1878, signed himself, "Pocatello."

Agent Danilson telegraphed the commissioner on September 22, 1878, the news that the Utah and Northern Railroad, projected from Ogden north to Montana, was preparing to advance its terminus to a ten-acre plat in the center of the reservation at what was to become the city of Pocatello. He asked what force he could use to stop any threats.[10] Mormon promoters had organized this narrow-gauge line in August 1871 to connect the Cache Valley settlements with Salt Lake City and perhaps to tap profits from the western Montana gold camps. The Panic of 1873 dried up construction funds so that work on the road ceased in 1874 when it reached Franklin in northern Cache Valley. The Union Pacific took over the railroad in 1877 and began extending it northward. By the summer of 1878 the railroad terminus was at the southern end of the Fort Hall Reservation, and by September Agent Danilson was facing a new station at "Pocatello." Chief Pocatello was receiving a recognition of sorts as people used his name for their own purposes.[11]

By the close of 1878 and months after the last Bannock warriors had been put to flight, killed, or captured, Captain Bainbridge completed a census account of the Indians at Fort Hall showing 154 Bannock (which did not include the 76 warriors confined at the military post) and 838 Shoshoni.[12] In his annual report for 1879, Danilson listed 331 Bannock and 888 Shoshoni but noted that 129 Bannock and 142 Shoshoni were absent from the reservation at the time of the count. It is possible that Pocatello was one of those away from the reservation. Danilson listed the number of acres under cultivation by Indian farmers: Bannock and Murshaw creeks, 147 acres; Port Neuf, 32 acres; Pocatellah, 5 acres; Emigrant Rock, 122 acres; Agency, 224 acres.[13] Could the hard-riding and far-ranging chief of yesteryear have settled down to plow and plant his five acres at "Pocatellah"? We will probably never know.

Until November 1881, no notice of Chief Pocatello appears in the correspondence or records of the Fort Hall agency. Apparently he spent most of his time on the reservation learning, as did the other Indians, a new way of life. When a group of the reservation leaders signed a petition on March 2, 1881, asking that the current agent, John A. Wright, be removed, Chief Pocatello's "His X Mark" does not appear on the list of the nineteen Shoshoni and seven Bannock chiefs and headmen. Captain Jim was first and Pocatello John third to sign for the Shoshoni. Chief Tihee was the first Bannock to affix his mark.[14] E. A. Stone, who was named temporary agent after Wright left, looked upon Gibson Jack as "the principal Shoshone chief" at the reservation.[15]

Continuing troubles with Union Pacific officials over the reservation right-of-way for the Utah and Northern Railroad and a second request for the east-west Oregon Short Line through the reservation resulted in two council meetings with the Shoshoni and Bannock to get their approval of the two lines. Again, Pocatello was notably absent from either meeting. The agreement of July 18, 1881, formalizing Union Pacific requests for the routes and including the cession of a strip of land two hundred feet wide at Pocatello Station was approved by 269 Indians. Jack Gibson signed in the number one spot followed by Pocatello Tom as number two and Pocatello John as number three. Far down the list was Pocatello Pete.[16]

One writer asserts that Pocatello John and Pocatello Pete were brothers of the original Pocatello,[17] but my research indicates that Pocatello John was not related but earned his prominent position through force of personality. Pocatello Tom and Pocatello Pete were evidently brothers or cousins of Pocatello. By 1881, the first Pocatello was being called "General Pocatello" to distinguish him from all the others by that name and, no doubt, to give him the prominence he deserved.[18]

General Pocatello did participate in one more important agreement with the government before his death. When the Fort Hall Reservation was set aside as a permanent home for the Shoshoni and Bannock by 1869, a number of Mormon farmers had already settled in the southern portion of the new reserve in Marsh Valley. They were understandably concerned about titles to their lands and kept up an unceasing agitation to have the southern portion of the reservation cut off so they could obtain title to their farms. Finally, a delegation of seven chiefs from Fort Hall traveled to Washington, D.C., in May 1881, where an agreement was reached on the cession

An unidentified member of the Shoshoni Pocatello band. *Marriott Library, University of Utah*.

and other matters. The seven leaders were Tendoy of the Lemhi, Tissidimit, Grouse Pete, Jack Gibson, Tihee, Captain Jim, and Jack Tendoy. The agreement had the following provisions: the Lemhi were to give up their small reservation on the Lemhi River and move to Fort Hall; the Shoshoni and Bannock at Fort Hall approved the cession of 325,000 acres in Marsh Valley in return for $120,000; and land allotments were to be made to individual families on the basis of 160 acres of farmland and another 160 acres of grazing land. The seven chiefs signed the agreement and returned home to present it to their tribes. [19]

On November 14, 1881, 250 Shoshoni and Bannock acceded to the agreement. The first ten marks were made by Jack Gibson, Captain Jim, Tihee, Jim Ballard, Race Horse, Major George, Pocatello John, Pedogo, Tasoacobynakse, and "Gen'l Pocatello" as number ten. Pocatello Pete appeared as number ninety-five; Pocatello Tom did not sign at all. [20] This apparently was the last appearance of General Pocatello in a major council as a recognized reservation leader. Incidentally, Congress did not ratify the cession agreement, with some changes, until February 23, 1889. Pocatello had died long before the slow-moving legislature got around to the agreement he had endorsed. [21]

Judge Walter Taylor Oliver has left an eyewitness account of Pocatello's death and burial. A native Virginian, Judge Oliver moved to Idaho in 1870, took possession of land along the south bank of the Snake River about ten miles above American Falls, and established the Oliver Tavern for travelers on the road to Oregon. According to Oliver, the chief and his family had been living in the lower foothills of Bannock Creek. In October 1884, after an extended illness and realizing he was going to die, Pocatello directed his wives and family to take him and his possessions to the Snake River bottoms, close to the Oliver ranch. One evening the judge heard the Indian women and children crying and upon investigation learned that the old chief had died. Pocatello had made preparations for his death and had brought his eighteen horses and his hunting equipment with him.

The day after the chief's death, Judge Oliver and his wife, the only white settlers within twenty-two miles, attended the final rites and assisted in the burial. Pocatello had directed that he be interred in a large spring of unknown depth and about twenty feet in diameter. The spring has since been covered to a depth of fifteen feet by the waters of the American Falls Reservoir. The Indians looked upon the spring as a sacred place. Judge Oliver then described his burial:

First we took the chief and wound all his clothing around him, then tied his guns, knives, and all his hunting equipment and relics to the clothing with willow thongs and tossed him out into the middle of the spring, and he went to the bottom quickly. Then the Indians took the eighteen head of horses, killed them one by one and rolled them into the spring on top of the old man, and they too were soon out of sight, for the spring is said to have no bottom.

In concluding his description of Pocatello's burial, Judge Oliver also reminisced:

As I remember Chief Pocatello he was about 70 years old, about 5 feet 10 inches tall, straight as a sapling and a pretty good-looking old man. He was always pleasant and I have spent many hours talking with him for he often came to see me and my wife, sort of liked us, sometimes he would stay three or four days and camp a few rods from my house.[22]

Perhaps it was fitting for Chief Pocatello to be interred in this unique way after such an original and free life.

Pocatello's first wife surfaced again in 1922. A news dispatch of the *Salt Lake Tribune* of October 5, 1922, noted that Man-a-witze, the only surviving wife of the three wives of the Indian leader had visited Brigham City from her home on Bannock Creek. She was 112 years old at the time, having reportedly been born in 1810. The reporter wrote, "She was the first wife of the noted chief, who reigned over the land at the time Brigham Young and his followers entered the valley in 1847. . . . Her recollections of the past are vivid, and she well remembers the time when the wild buffalo roved over this land and the Mormons made their entrance in 1847."[23] Pocatello might have been pleased to learn that he had "reigned" over his homeland.

Pocatello's life and career can be divided into six segments. From his birth around 1815 to the end of the fur trade era in 1840 when emigrants began to throng the western roads, Pocatello and his people lived in what Sven Liljeblad has called the "golden age" of their history. Furnished with firearms and cooking utensils and with their game, grass seeds, and roots still undisturbed by white men and large cattle herds, the Northwestern Shoshoni lived well.

During this period, Pocatello's band may have hunted buffalo on the Snake River plains near the Portneuf River and traded with the fur companies who came in looking for beaver skins. By 1840 also, Pocatello was beginning to exert leadership talents by taking command of his own people at Grouse Creek and that of other Shoshoni north of Great Salt Lake and on Bannock Creek.

With the coming of the Mormon settlers in 1847 and their appropriation of Indian lands and water, Pocatello began to feel the restricting pressures that would eventually result in the loss of his homeland. At the same time, his position at the junction of the California Trail and the Salt Lake Road placed him in the midst of emigrant traffic to the Pacific Coast, especially during the gold-rush years when as many as 70,000 travelers surged through his district. Not only did the argonauts destroy game and grass cover, some of the more irresponsible killed his tribesmen in wanton attacks, bringing swift retaliation from the chief and his angry warriors. When Frederick Lander met the young chief in 1859, he was much impressed and noted the moderation with which he had responded to white attacks on his people. While the Mormon settlers had advanced as far north as Brigham City by this time, they were still on the edge of Northwestern Shoshoni territory and had not yet overwhelmed Indian subsistence areas.

A third period, from 1859 to 1864, marked dramatic changes for Pocatello. First, Mormon farmers soon took possession of all Cache Valley and were even in Malad Valley. Second, as a result of the Utah War, all at once there was a large U.S. Army contingent stationed at Camp Floyd that soon demonstrated its power by capturing Pocatello and placing him in irons for very little reason. When these troops left with the coming of the Civil War, Col. Patrick E. Connor and his California Volunteers soon replaced them and engaged Chief Bear Hunter and other Cache Valley chiefs in a battle that deteriorated into the Bear River Massacre and that Pocatello escaped by only one day. In the aftermath, Connor tried to hunt down the Northwestern chief but succeeded only in getting him to the bargaining table to sign the Treaty of Box Elder in July 1863. Later, the general and the chief tried to stare each other down in a confrontation at Camp Douglas, where Pocatello had been made prisoner as a result of charges made against him by the "Stagecoach King," Ben Holladay. This military period in Pocatello's career taught him a healthy respect for the troops, but did not diminish his independent spirit.

Faced with a terrible loss of subsistence in the late 1860s, Pocatello joined the Washakie and Tahgee buffalo hunts into Wyoming and Montana during the winters of 1867 to 1869 to return in the last year to yet three more events which had a great impact upon him and his tribe. The first of these, the establishment of the Fort Hall Reservation, meant the eventual end to his wanderings and a confining home at Bannock Creek. The completion of the transcontinental railroad right through his homeland north of the Promontory Mountains resulted in the establishment of Corinne, a non-Mormon town that was to prove anathema to him and his people. All of these events brought in more white settlers and led him to try living at Fort Hall, but the experience proved frustrating and life threatening as a neglectful government failed to provide the funds to feed the Indians on the new reserve. It was during this period when we begin to get the key to Pocatello's later career as a resident at Fort Hall. Agent High's observation that although recognized by his followers as head chief and even willing to perform the leadership duties, he declined the honor of the title and office, preferring to let such strong men as Pocatello John deal with the bureaucracy and politics of reservation life.

The Powell-Ingalls Commission finally committed the government to placing all the Northwestern Shoshoni on the Fort Hall Reservation, declaring an end to their wanderings among the Mormon settlements of northern Utah. But the starving times at the reservation introduced a final chapter in Pocatello's story, when Mormon missionary George Hill's farm on the lower Bear River offered one last hope for the beleagured Shoshoni. The "Corinne Indian Scare" defeated that endeavor even though the pragmatic Pocatello had demanded baptism in the LDS Church to ensure his share of the emoluments Hill's "reservation" farm provided. Disillusioned by the failure of the Mormons to stand up to the troops from Fort Douglas, the apostate Pocatello returned to an uncertain future at Fort Hall.

During the last nine years of his life, he lived at Bannock Creek, removed some twenty-five miles from the agency at Fort Hall. He may have tried his hand at farming, but it is more likely that he spent most of his time traveling back to his old home at Grouse Creek and elsewhere searching for food and following the habits of a long life. His rather original burial in a large spring just north of Bannock Creek concluded a life of resolute courage, fierce independence, and outstanding leadership.

His relationships with emigrants, Mormon settlers, U.S. troops, and government officials, gained him notoriety for outlawry and intransigence not altogether justified by the circumstances. In a day when Indian leaders were expected to show obeisance to the supposedly superior white men, Pocatello's boldness did not indicate a respectful attitude toward the presiding authorities. His audacity in demanding and expecting help from the interlopers who were taking over his homeland brought condemnation and exasperation from the army officers and other officials who had to deal with him. And the intolerant and sanguinary frontier newspaper editors of the day were quick to establish an aura of recalcitrance around Pocatello.

How does Pocatello fit into western history? Unlike Utah Indian leaders Walker, Black Hawk, or Bear Hunter, or the Wyoming Chief Washakie, who resided in the well-watered and sheltered valleys of the Wasatch and Wind River ranges, Pocatello was a border chieftain wandering the sagebrush deserts along the boundary of Utah and Idaho. Operating on the northern fringe of Mormon settlement and at the junction of the California Trail and the Salt Lake Road, he became a shadowy and elusive character who showed up at opportunistic moments only to disappear again into his desert environment. His propensity to go his own way marked him as an aloof figure who dealt with whites only when he chose. He was a brigand and a warrior, a strategist and a diplomat, a legendary but tragic figure, a hobgoblin at times, and always an unfettered leader of courage and determination.

His life was transitional. His antagonists could outmaneuver him, but always he survived. His toughness of spirit and tenaciousness were born of the desert habitat which nurtured him. He could react with disgust and anger at the injustices and deceits of the white man's exploitation of his people, but he always endured, scouring the desert for the next meal and maintaining a youthfulness of spirit until reservation life forced him into seclusion on Bannock Creek. He refused to collaborate with the government agents although he could join up with the Mormons when food and lodging beckoned. When the starving time came to Fort Hall, he reverted to his lifelong habits of mobility by joining Washakie and Tahgee in search of buffalo on the plains of Wyoming. Leading his young men against the Sioux raiding parties represented his last fling at his old trade of war chief before succumbing to the inevitable sequestered life on a reservation.

No one ever put a brand on him. Perhaps the Mormons came the closest when he agreed to be baptized so as to gain access to the benefits of George Hill's farm. But the conversion lasted only a few months. Chief Pocatello was a free spirit who roamed his beloved plains and mountains, hunted the buffalo, fought the Sioux, raided Ben Holladay's stage stations, and struck terror into the hearts of western travelers and farmers alike. Perhaps it is quite fitting that his name has been given to the second largest city in Idaho, located where he once pitched his tipi.

8

Epilogue

How the name Pocatello came to be attached to the present city is an interesting exercise in historical study. By the end of the fur trade era in 1840, most geographic names had already been established in the Fort Hall area—Snake River, Blackfoot River, Portneuf River, Ross Fork, etc. But apparently a small creek that flows from the hills in a westerly direction right through the center of the present city into the Portneuf River did not gain a permanent name during this time. Quite probably, Chief Pocatello habitually camped for a length of time each year at the confluence of the creek and the Portneuf River, so it gained the name of Pocatello's Creek.

When the Montana Trail came to be definitely marked as a result of the gold discoveries in the Beaverhead country after 1862, the new route crossed Pocatello Creek. The early stagecoach companies established a station at the crossing with the natural name of Pocatello Station being attached to the post. By 1868, *The Direct Route, to Colorado, Idaho, Utah, Montana, Nevada and California* listed Pocatello as a swing station on the Wells Fargo & Co. stage route to Montana. It was located thirteen miles beyond Black Rock Station and twelve miles from Ross Fork Station, which was a home station. [1]

After the Utah and Northern Railroad crossed the Fort Hall Reservation in 1878, the Union Pacific Railroad began to make plans for the Oregon Short Line to Portland that would branch off from the Utah and Northern Railroad at Pocatello Station. Realizing the importance of the junction of the two roads, the Union

Pacific received an agreement from the Shoshoni and Bannock on July 8, 1881, for a right-of-way across the reservation including a cession of forty acres of ground at Pocatello Station. By another agreement in 1887, the Indians increased the allotment at Pocatello to 1,840 acres and the city of Pocatello was on its way.[2] Soon, the railroad shops that had been at Eagle Rock (now Idaho Falls) were moved to Pocatello at the junction of the south-north and east-west lines of the Union Pacific.

Of equal interest in trying to establish how a city came to be named for Chief Pocatello is attempting to discover what the Indian leader looked like. He seems as elusive here as he was when General Connor was trying to capture him. There is no known photograph of him, although there are a lot of photographs of other prominent Indians at Fort Hall including Pocatello John, Pocatello Pete, and Pocatello Tom. There is a supposed likeness of the chief in the form of a medallion for the participants in the Fifth Annual Pharmaceutical Convention held in the city of Pocatello on May 10 and 11, 1911. J. P. Halliwell of the Halliwell Drug Store had the medallion prepared which "bears the likeness of an Indian (apparently taken from a photograph) with the caption in small but clear letters: 'Chief Pocatello.'" Also, sometime early in this century, the Franklin & Hayes Brewing Co. of Pocatello, Idaho, evidently used the same likeness as a trademark on a metal serving tray advertising the Carnation "Bud" bottled beer they sold. It was reported that Charles H. Russell, the famous western artist, was commissioned to design the trademark and that he apparently used the medallion likeness for his portrayal of Chief Pocatello or vice versa.[3] A comparison of the known photograph of Pocatello Tom shows a startling similarity to the picture of his brother, Chief Pocatello, and it is quite possible that Charles Russell or the unknown artist who prepared the medallion likeness used Pocatello Tom's photograph as a model. Perhaps it was as close as the portraitist could come in capturing the original Pocatello.[4] Apparently, we shall have to be satisfied with this picture of Pocatello as a beer salesman just as more prominent American leaders have had their names attached to life insurance companies and birthday sales.

In an effort to celebrate the now famous Pocatello, Dr. and Mrs. N. W. Christiansen, in 1953, published a series of musical compositions entitled, *A Trip Through Yellowstone Park: Interesting Events Portrayed in Music,* including among seventeen numbers one about Chief Pocatello. Songs were devoted to "Fishing Bridge," "Old Faithful," "Dog Races at Ashton," and one was called "Cowboy Dance." The two verses for the "Chief Pocatello" composition, which has a rather tom-tom beat, are as follows:

> Po-ca-tel-lo heap big Indian
> Tell me what you do.
> Where's your wigwam, where's your cayuse,
> Are you big Chief too?
>
> Me big chief called Po-ca-tel-lo
> Tell you what I do.
> Hunt all day with bow and arrow
> Shoot the big bear Too Ki-yi![5]

Notes

1. PROLOGUE

1. Minnie F. Howard, "Pocatello's Mother," *Idaho Yesterday and Today*, pp. 22–25; Jeannette Lewis, "The Story of Widzhebu (A Cunning Eye)," pp. 1–10; Sven Liljeblad, "Indian Peoples in Idaho," p. 114.

2. INTRODUCTION

1. William Stearns Davis, *A History of France*, p. 124.

2. Thomas Babington Macaulay, *Miscellaneous*, vol. 3, p. 287.

3. Brigham D. Madsen, *The Northern Shoshoni*, pp. 17–29; Brigham D. Madsen, *The Shoshoni Frontier and the Bear River Massacre*, introduction.

4. Madsen, *Shoshoni Frontier*, Introduction.

5. Ibid.; Brigham D. Madsen, *The Bannock of Idaho*, chap. 1.

6. Brigham D. Madsen, *The Lemhi: Sacajawea's People*, chaps. 1–5.

7. Madsen, *The Shoshoni Frontier*, introduction; Madsen, *The Northern Shoshoni*, pp. 43–48, 53–56.

8. Madsen, *The Shoshoni Frontier*, introduction.

9. Ibid.

10. Anthropologist Sven Liljeblad has also provided information for the Idaho Historical Society's Reference Series no. 484, November 1970, "Shoshoni and Northern Paiute Indians in Idaho." This statement is evidently the most accurate analysis of Shoshoni bands now available and is the result of his many years of study of Shoshoni groups.

11. Brigham D. Madsen, "The Northwestern Shoshoni in Cache Valley," in Douglas D. Alder, ed., *Cache Valley: Essays on Her Past and People*, pp. 28–44.

12. Julian Steward, *Basin-Plateau Aboriginal Sociopolitical Groups*, pp. 136, 149. See also Ake Hultkrantz, "The Shoshones in the Rocky Mountain Area" in *Shoshone Indians*, pp. 22–24 and Liljeblad, "Indian Peoples in Idaho," pp. 111–14.

13. Merle Wells, Letter, Boise, Idaho, Feb. 28, 1985.

14. U.S. Dept. of the Interior, *Annual Report to the Commissioner of Indian Affairs, 1859* (hereinafter referred to as *Annual Report*), Forney to the Commissioner of Indian Affairs (hereinafter referred to as CIA), Sept. 29, 1859, No. 174, p. 363.

15. Liljeblad, "Indian Peoples in Idaho," pp. 54–56; Hultkrantz, "The Shoshones in the Rocky Mountain Area," pp. 22–24; Steward, *Basin-Plateau Aboriginal Groups*, pp. 173–75.

16. Merle Wells interview with Sven Liljeblad, Reno, Nevada, June 29, 1984.

17. Howard Ross Cramer, *California-Oregon Trail: Fort Hall to Goose Creek, Idaho*, p. 4.

18. L. A. Fleming and A. R. Standing, "The Road to 'Fortune': The Salt Lake Cutoff," *Utah Historical Quarterly* 33 (Summer 1965)3: 250–61; Lorenzo Sawyer, *Way Sketches*, pp. 66; *U.S. Dept. of the Interior Annual Report 1855*, Garland Hurt to CIA, Sept. 30, 1855, pp. 157–201; *Deseret News*, Sept. 5, 1855; Interview with Sven Liljeblad, Reno, Nev., June 29, 1984.

19. Milton R. Hunter, *Brigham Young, The Colonizer*, pp. 290–95.

20. Brigham D. Madsen, *Gold Rush Sojourners in Great Salt Lake City*, p. 33.

21. Ibid.; John D. Unruh, Jr., *The Plains Across*, pp. 119–20.

3. FROM GROUSE CREEK TO A CHIEFTAINSHIP

1. La Salle Pocatello, Interview, p. 10; Jeannette Pocatello believed that Pocatello's natural father was Shoshoni. Interview with Sven Liljeblad, Reno, Nev., June 29, 1984.

2. Julian Steward, *Basin-Plateau Aboriginal Groups*, p. 212.

3. Frederick W. Lander to CIA, Feb. 18, 1860, National Archives (hereinafter referred to as NA), Letters Received, 1824–1881, M234, Utah Superintendency, 1849–1880, roll 899, 29; Walter Taylor Oliver, "The Burial of Chief Pocatello," in *Idaho Yesterday and Today*, p. 26.

4. Dimick B. Huntington, Journal, 1857–58–59. Huntington had been a long-time member of the LDS Church having joined in 1836. He had moved with the church to Kirtland, Ohio, and then to Caldwell County, Missouri, where he served as a deputy sheriff. After participating in the Battle of Crooked River, he escaped to Ilinois and later became a member of the Mormon Battalion. His career in Utah was marked by years of service as an Indian interpreter and guide.

5. Lander to CIA, Feb. 18, 1860, p. 14.

6. Lewis, "The Story of Widzhebu," p. 9.

7. Randy Stapilus and O. K. Johnson, "Fort Hall—A State of Transition, 1868–1979," *Idaho State Journal*.

8. Interview with Merle W. Wells, Dec. 20, 1983; Robert M. Weir, *Colonial South Carolina: A History*, p. 84; Merrill D. Beal in his *A History of Southeastern Idaho* wrote that Pocatello "was a corpulent Indian, and French trappers called him 'pork and tallow,' which was finally corrupted to Pokatello." In his footnote to the above, Beal added, "Frank Miller's notes. Miller obtained this information from Mrs. Lavoda, a stepchild of the chief, on June 26, 1930."

9. Liljeblad, "Indian Peoples in Idaho," p. 1; Lewis, "The Story of Widzhebu," p. 9; see also H. Leigh Gittins, *Pocatello Portrait: The Early Years, 1878 to 1928*, p. 21; Interview with Liljeblad, Reno, Nev., Feb. 28, 1985.

10. Liljeblad, "Indian Peoples in Idaho," p. 49.

11. The descriptions of the food habits and migrations of the Grouse Creek Shoshoni are based on the excellent studies by Steward and Liljeblad: Steward,

Basin-Plateau Aboriginal Groups, pp. 173–77; Liljeblad, "Indian Peoples in Idaho," pp. 34–49, 54–56, 111–15.

12. Merle W. Wells, Letter, Boise, Idaho, February 28, 1985.

13. Steward, *Basin-Plateau Aboriginal Groups,* pp. 174–77, 216–18.

14. David Moore, Journal and Life History, pp. 8–9.

15. Ibid., pp. 10–11; *Portland Oregonian,* May 1, 1852; Brown to Fullmer, n.d., Wells to McBride, Sept. 17, 1850, Wells to Fullmer, Sept. 17, 1850, Wells to Eldredge, Sept. 17, 1850, Wells to Ward, Sept. 17, 1850, Wells to Eldredge, Sept. 18, 1850, Eldredge to Ferguson, Sept. 20, 1850, and Daniel H. Wells, General Orders, Sept. 18, 1850, all in Utah State Militia Correspondence, 1849–63.

16. Wells to Robinson, Sept. 19, 1850, Utah State Militia Correspondence, 1849–63.

17. Wells to Kimball, Sept. 25, 1860, ibid.

18. Moore, Journal and Life History, p. 4; Clark to Canfield, July 8, 1851, Utah Territorial Papers. Brigham Young, Manuscript History, July 10, 1851, p. 5.

19. Holeman to CIA, Apr. 29, 1852, and Young to CIA, May 25, 1852, NA, Letters Received, Utah Superintendency, roll 897.

20. Brigham Young, Indian Affairs, Correspondence, 1851–53, folder 16, September 25, 1852.

21. Moore to Wells, Aug. 29, 1853, Utah State Militia Correspondence, 1849–63.

22. Ibid.

23. Elijah Nicholas Wilson, *Among the Shoshones,* pp. 23–31.

24. Brigham Young, Manuscript History, Sept. 4, 1854, p. 83.

25. Brigham Young, Journal History, Aug. 23, 1855.

26. Brigham Young, Indian Affairs, Miscellaneous Licenses, Permits, etc., 1854–1856, folder 30, Jan. 15, 1855.

27. Hurt to Young, Sept. 30, 1855, *Annual Report, 1855,* pp. 199–200.

28. Ibid.; *Deseret News,* Sept. 12, 1844.

29. A. J. Simmonds, The First Settlements, 1855–1860, pp. 4–7.

30. Young, Journal History, July 24, 1856.

31. For a concise summary of the Utah War, see Eugene E. Campbell, "Governmental Beginnings," in *Utah's History,* pp. 165–70.

32. Huntington, Journal, Aug. 10, 1857.

33. Ibid., Aug. 11, 1857.

34. Ibid., Sept. 30, 1857.

35. Ibid.

36. Young to CIA, Sept. 12, 1857, Utah Superintendency, roll 898.

37. Huntington, Journal, May 3, 1858.

38. Brigham Young, Papers, 1801–77, Maughan to Young, October 27, 1857.

4. MORMON SETTLERS AND ARMY TROOPS

1. Forney to CIA, Sept. 23, 1858, NA, Letters Received: Utah Superintendency, roll 898.

2. Forney to CIA, Sept. 29, 1859, *Annual Report, 1859,* 731.

3. Forney to CIA, Nov. 5, 1858, ibid.

4. *Deseret News,* Aug. 10, 1859.

5. Ibid.; *Annual Report, 1859,* 741; Young, Journal History, Aug. 9, 1859, 1.

6. Young, Journal History, Aug. 9; *Deseret News,* Aug. 10, 1859.

7. *National Cyclopaedia of American Biography,* p. 127.

8. U.S. Congress, Senate, *Message of the President of the United States,* Lander to Forney, Aug. 16, 1859, pp. 28–29.

9. Ibid., Gay to Porter, Camp on Bear River, Aug. 17, 1859.

10. Ibid., Lynde to Porter, Aug. 26, 1859.

11. Wilson, *Among the Shoshones,* pp. 117, 132.

12. Lander to CIA, Feb. 18, 1860, NA, Letters Received: Utah Superintendency, roll 899. An unsubstantiated story in the *American Falls Press* of Mar. 4, 1915, reported another possible reason for Pocatello's dislike of emigrants: "General Pocatello was a silent Indian and could not become friendly to the whites. The probable reason for this was the dealing out, by a party of emigrants, of summary justice to a band of Shoshones. It was about 1860 that a band of Indians were harrassing [*sic*] an immigrant train on the Truckee river in Nevada. The immigrants were too strong for the Indians and captured one of them. Fastening the tongues of three wagons together, so as to make a tripod, they hanged the captured Indian, who happened to be Pocatello's father. Whatever Pocatello's conduct up to that time had been, he at once became an implacable foe of the whites."

13. George R. Stewart, *The California Trail,* pp. 323–24.

14. James Bywater, Reminiscences, folder 923, no. 7.

15. "Massacre Rocks," Idaho State Historical Society, Reference Series, No. 234. Revised 1985.

16. Interview with Sven Liljeblad, Reno, Nev., June 29, 1984.

17. "Massacre Rocks," Idaho State Historical Society, Reference Series, No. 234.

18. Ibid. This well-researched and well-written summation of the Massacre Rocks engagements by the staff of the Idaho State Historical Society includes relevant excerpts from diaries, journals, letters, and newspaper accounts: Henry M. Judson, Diary of 1862, Omaha to Oregon, Nebraska State Historical Society #358, MS 953; Hamilton Scott, Diary; John C. Hilman, Letter to Mrs. Bronson, Aug. 11, 1862, included in Hamilton Scott, Diary; H. F. Swasley, Letter to *Quincy Union* (Illinois), Oct. 28, 1862; Report in *Silver Age* (Carson City) as reprinted in *San Francisco Evening Bulletin,* Sept. 27, 1862; William Redhener, Journal, excerpt printed in *Washington Statesman* (Walla Walla), Oct. 4, 1862, p. 2, E-5; Charles H. Harrison, Report to *State Press* (Iowa City) as reprinted in *Idaho World* (Idaho City), Mar. 31, 1911, p. 1, C. 6–7; and Captain Medorem Crawford, Commander of the 1862 Emigrant Service, in a letter to the Secretary of War.

19. Doty to CIA, Apr. 15, 1862, NA, Letters Received: Utah Superintendency, roll 900.

20. Don Richard Mathis, "Camp Floyd in Retrospect," pp. 139–42.

21. Richard H. Orton, comp., *Records of California Men in the War of Rebellion, 1861 to 1867,* p. 12.

22. Fred B. Rogers, *Soldiers of the Overland,* pp. 1–4.

23. *Deseret News,* Oct. 22, 1862; U.S. Congress, House, *The War of the Rebellion,* vol. L, part 1, p. 195.

24. U.S. Congress, House, *The War of the Rebellion*, vol. L, part 2, pp. 178–79.

25. *Sacramento Union*, Dec. 26, 1862; James H. Martineau, "The Military History of Cache County," *Tullidge's Quarterly Magazine* 2 (April 1882)1: 125; Newell Hart, "Rescue of a Frontier Boy," *Utah Historical Quarterly* 33 (Winter 1965)1: 51–54.

26. *Deseret News*, Dec. 17, 19, 1862; *Sacramento Union*, Dec. 26, 1862.

27. Betty M. Madsen and Brigham D. Madsen, *North to Montana*, p. 23.

28. U.S. Congress, House, *Report of the Secretary of the Interior*, serial no. 1157, 1862, pp. 536–37.

29. *Deseret News*, Jan. 14, 1863; *Sacramento Union*, Jan. 26, 1863.

30. *Sacramento Union*, Jan. 31, 1863; *Deseret News*, Jan. 28, 1863; Newell Hart, *The Bear River Massacre*, p. 112; Lyman Clarence Pedersen, Jr., "History of Fort Douglas, Utah," p. 55; U.S. Congress, House, *The War of the Rebellion*, vol. L, part I, p. 187.

31. Mae T. Parry, "Massacre at Boa Ogoi" in Newell Hart, ed., *The Trail Blazer*, p. 129.

32. Ibid.; Hart, *The Bear River Massacre*, p. 264.

33. See Brigham D. Madsen, *The Shoshoni Frontier*, chap. 10, pp. 34–36, for an account of the "Battle." Interview with Sven Liljeblad, Reno, Nev., June 29, 1984; see also Edward J. Barta, "Battle Creek: The Battle of Bear River."

34. Hart, *The Bear River Massacre*, pp. 201, 259.

35. *Deseret News*, May 20, 1868.

36. U.S. Congress, House, *The War of the Rebellion*, vol. L, part I, p. 187; *San Francisco Bulletin*, Feb. 20, 1863; *Alta California*, Feb. 19, 1863.

37. Roskelley to Benson and Maughan, Feb. 8, 1863, Brigham Young, Papers, 1801–77.

38. *Deseret News*, Apr. 22, 1863.

39. Ibid., May 13, 1863.

40. U.S. Congress, House, *Report of the Secretary of the Interior*, serial no. 1182, 1863, pp. 515–16.

41. Madsen, *The Northern Shoshoni*, pp. 36–37.

42. Doty to CIA, July 6, 1863, NA, Letters Received: Utah Superintendency, roll 901.

43. Nichols to Doty, July 11, 1863, NA, Utah Superintendency Files (field records), Misc. 1862–63–64, unprinted record.

44. U.S. Congress, House, *The War of the Rebellion*, vol. L, part II, p. 529.

45. Charles J. Kappler, *Indian Affairs: Laws and Treaties*, vol. 2, pp. 848–51; Doty to CIA, July 1863, NA, Letters Received: Utah Superintendency, roll 901.

46. *Deseret News*, Aug. 5, 1863.

47. Madsen, *The Northern Shoshoni*, p. 37.

48. Doty to CIA, Nov. 10, 1863, *Annual Report, 1864*, p. 319.

49. Maughan to Young, July 28, 1864, Young, Papers, 1801–77.

50. John Henry Evans, *Charles Coulson Rich: Pioneer Builder of the West*, pp. 259–60.

51. Statement of Paul Coburn, Salt Lake City, Oct. 22, 1864, NA, Letters Received by the Adjutant General's Office, 1861–70, Microfilm M619, roll 267, pp. 566–67. For an interesting report of the incident, see Jeffery King, "'Do Not

Execute Chief Pocatello': President Lincoln Acts to Save the Shoshoni Chief," *Utah Historical Quarterly* 53 (Summer 1985)3: 237–47.

52. Irish to Dole, Oct. 29, 1864, NA, *Letters Received by the Adjutant General's Office, 1861–70*, p. 559.

53. Ibid., pp. 559–61.

54. Irish to Connor, Salt Lake City, Oct. 27, 1864, ibid., pp. 547–57.

55. Irish to Dole, ibid., pp. 559–65.

56. Connor to Irish, Nov. 4, 1863, NA, Letters Received: Utah Superintendency, roll 901.

57. Irish to Dole, Nov. 9, 1863, ibid.

58. Irish to Dole, Nov. 22, 1862, and Doty to Dole, Nov. 25, 1863, ibid.

59. Dole to Usher, Nov. 25, 1863, NA, *Letters Received by the Adjutant General's Office, 1861–70*, pp. 545–46.

60. Ibid.; Dole to Irish, November 26, 1864, NA, *Letters Sent*, roll 75, p. 471.

5. A RESERVATION AND A RAILROAD

1. Coburn to Irish, Apr. 16, 1865, NA, Letters Received: Utah Superintendency, roll 901.

2. Irish to Coburn, Apr. 28, 1865, and Irish to Dole, Apr. 28, 1865, ibid.

3. Brigham Young, Journal History, July 26, 1865.

4. Irish to Cooley, Oct. 9, 1865, NA, Letters Received: Utah Superintendency, roll 901.

5. *Deseret News,* Nov. 2, 1865.

6. Gov. of Idaho to Turner, Dec. 10, 1865, NA, Territorial Papers, Idaho: 1864–90, M191, roll 3.

7. *Annual Report, 1866,* 122–23; ibid., p. 188.

8. Young, Manuscript History, Mar. 11, 1866, p. 180.

9. *Annual Report, 1867,* p. 188; Head to CIA, June 10, 1867, NA, Letters Received: Utah Superintendency, roll 902.

10. *Annual Report, 1868,* p. 153.

11. Head to CIA, Jan. 4, 1868, NA, Letters Received: Utah Superintendency, roll 902.

12. *Annual Report, 1868,* p. 151.

13. Young, Journal History, May 7, 1868, p. 2.

14. See Brigham D. Madsen, *The Northern Shoshoni,* for a detailed account of the efforts to establish the Fort Hall Reservation, pp. 48–56.

15. White to Ballard, May 8, 1868, NA, Miscellaneous Sources, 1864 and 1866–69, Idaho Superintendency, roll 2.

16. Brigham D. Madsen, *The Northern Shoshoni,* pp. 53–58.

17. Powell to Ballard, Jan. 14, 1869, Miscellaneous Sources, roll 2.

18. Powell to Ballard, Apr. 26, 1869, ibid.

19. Young, Journal History, May 10, 1869, p. 11.

20. Madsen, *The Northern Shoshoni,* pp. 53–58.

21. Powell to Ballard, June 30, 1869, NA, Letters Received, 1824–1881, M234, Idaho Superintendency, 1863–80, roll 338; Parker to Floyd-Jones, Aug. 24, 1869, NA, Field Papers, Idaho Superintendency, p. 688.

22. *Annual Report, 1869,* pp. 729–30.

23. Tourtellotte to CIA, Dec. 3, 1869, NA, Letters Received: Utah Superintendency, roll 902.

24. *Deseret News,* July 20, 1869; Young, Journal History, July 17, 1869, p. 1.

25. Young, Journal History, July 25, 1869, p. 6.

26. Hart, *The Bear River Massacre,* p. 321.

27. Merrill D. Beal, *Intermountain Railroads,* chap. 10.

28. Brigham D. Madsen, *Corinne: The Gentile Capital of Utah,* pp. 5–11.

29. *Utah Reporter,* Oct. 23, 1869; Apr. 28, July 30, 31, 1870.

30. Fleming to Campbell, June 14, 1870, NA, Letters Received, Wyoming, p. 728.

31. L. L. Pohnanteer affidavit, June 18, 1870, Brigham Young, Indian Affairs, Misc. Papers, 1866–1873, folder 60.

32. Huntington to Parker, Dec. 20, 1870, NA, Letters Received: Utah Superintendency, roll 903.

33. Danilson to Walker, NA, *Field Papers, Idaho Superintendency,* p. 705.

34. Danilson to Floyd-Jones, July 9, Aug. 26, 1870, Fort Hall Letter Book, pp. 44, 48–49.

35. Floyd-Jones, "Talk with the Indians in Council at Ft Hall," NA, Letters Received: Idaho Superintendency, roll 2.

36. *Annual Report, 1870,* p. 605.

37. *Corinne Reporter,* Nov. 16, 1870.

38. Ibid., Nov. 17, 1870.

39. Charles J. Kappler, *Statutes at Large,* vol. 16, p. 352.

40. *Corinne Reporter,* Jan. 6, Feb. 8, Mar. 22, 27, Apr. 6, June 10, 24, July 1, 15, 22, 26, 29, 30, Aug. 5, 19, 26, Nov. 17, 1871.

41. Ibid., Feb. 14, 1871.

42. Ibid., Feb. 15, 1871.

43. Ibid., June 17, 1871.

44. Berry to CIA, July 10, 1871, NA, Letters Received: Idaho Superintendency, roll 339.

45. *Corinne Journal,* July 15, 1871.

46. Berry to CIA, July 8, 1871, Fort Hall Letter Book, p. 383.

47. Hatch to Critchlow, Feb. 10, 1871, NA, Letters Received: Utah Superintendency, roll 903.

48. Berry to CIA, Nov. 24, 1871, NA, Letters Received: Idaho Superintendency, roll 339.

49. Berry to CIA, October 13, 1871, Fort Hall Letter Book, p. 92.

50. *Annual Report, 1872,* pp. 678–79.

51. Dodge to CIA, Jan. 6, 1872, NA, Letters Received: Utah Superintendency, roll 903.

52. Dodge to CIA, Feb. 2, 1872, ibid.

53. Dodge to CIA, Mar. 18, 1872, ibid.

54. Dodge to CIA, Apr. 20, 1872, ibid.

55. Dodge to CIA, July 24, 1872, ibid.

56. *Fourth Annual Report of the Board of Indian Commissioners to the President of the United States,* pp. 82–86.

57. Dodge to CIA, Aug. 16, 1872, NA, Letters Received: Utah Superintendency, roll 903.

58. Dodge to CIA, Oct. 28, 1872, ibid.

59. Dodge to CIA, Dec. 11, 1872, ibid.; Dodge to CIA, Dec. 26, 1872, ibid., roll 904.

60. Merle W. Wells, Letter, Boise, Idaho, Feb. 28, 1985.

61. High to CIA, Dec. 5, 1872, Fort Hall Letter Book, pp. 133–34.

62. *Corinne Reporter*, Apr. 30, 1873; see also the same newspaper for Mar. 14, Sept. 18, Nov. 23, 1872; Feb. 12, Mar. 20, Apr. 4, 5, 10, 14, 16, 29, May 7, 1873.

6. A STARVING TIME AND A RELIGIOUS EXPERIENCE

1. *Annual Report, 1873,* pp. 386, 409–10.

2. Ingalls to CIA, June 13, 1873, NA, Letters Received: Utah Superintendency, roll 904.

3. Powell to CIA, June 18, 1873, ibid.

4. Smith to Powell, June 25, 1873, ibid.

5. See also Young, Journal History, Nov. 8, 1873.

6. *Annual Report, 1873,* pp. 415–17.

7. U.S. Congress, House, *Statement of Major J. W. Powell,* January 13, 1874, p. 3.

8. Brigham D. Madsen, *The Northern Shoshoni,* pp. 69–70; U.S. Congress, House, *Bannock and Other Indians in Southern Idaho,* pp. 2–7. Congress never ratified the Agreement of 1873.

9. *Idaho Statesman,* Aug. 29, 1874.

10. Pagwite et al. to CIA, Aug. 30, 1874, NA, Letters Received, Idaho, 1865–1889, Indian Claims Commission, *Shoshone Indians, et al. v. United States,* Petitioners Exhibit no. 255.

11. Wright to CIA, Nov. 21, 1874, NA, Letters Received: Idaho Superintendency, roll 342.

12. Wright to CIA, Dec. 28, 1874, Fort Hall Letter Book, p. 205.

13. Charles E. Dibble, "The Mormon Mission to the Shoshoni Indians," *Western Humanities Review* 1 (1947): 284–85; Laurence G. Coates, "A History of Indian Education by the Mormons, 1830–1900," pp. 304–6; Ralph O. Brown, "The Life and Missionary Labors of George Washington Hill," pp. 59–65; the word Lamanite is a Book of Mormon term referring to the uncivilized portion of the American Indians.

14. Hill to CIA, Dec. 14, 1874, NA, Letters Received: Utah Superintendency, roll 904.

15. *Corinne Daily Mail,* Sept. 15, 28, Oct. 2, 5, 1874.

16. Ibid., Oct. 6, 1874.

17. Young, Journal History, Nov. 12, 1874; *Corinne Daily Mail,* Dec. 15, 1874.

18. *Corinne Daily Mail,* Dec. 10, 14, 21, 1874.

19. Wright to CIA, Jan. 30, 1875, Fort Hall Letter Book, p. 229; Wright to CIA, Feb. 6, 1875, ibid., p. 233.

20. *Corinne Daily Mail,* Jan. 6, Mar. 12, Apr. 15, 1875.

21. Dibble, "The Mormon Mission to the Shoshoni Indians," p. 285.

22. *Deseret News,* July 28, 1875; *Salt Lake Herald,* July 21, 1875.

23. Brigham Young, Papers, President's Office, Miscellaneous Papers, "July 1875 Lamanite Baptisms in May June and July 1875," roll 103, box 72, folder 1.

24. Dibble, "The Mormon Mission to the Shoshoni Indians," pp. 285–86.

25. George W. Hill, Collection, film 45, no. 6.

26. Wright to CIA, June 10, 1875, Fort Hall Letter Book, pp. 280–81.

27. George W. Hill, Collection, film 45, no. 6; the endowment ceremony is a ritual now performed in the LDS temples which "seals" families together for "time and eternity."

28. Wright to CIA, June 30, 1875, Fort Hall Letter Book, p. 284.

29. Danilson to CIA, July 31, 1875, ibid., p. 290.

30. Danilson to CIA, Sept. 1, 1875, ibid., pp. 298–99; *Annual Report, 1875,* p. 547.

31. *Corinne Daily Mail,* July 9, 19, 1875.

32. For a full report on the "Corinne Indian Scare," see Brigham D. Madsen, *Corinne: The Gentile Capital of Utah,* pp. 281–89; see also *Deseret News,* Aug. 18, Sept. 1, 1875; *Salt Lake Tribune,* Aug. 20, 1875; *Salt Lake Herald,* Aug. 17, 1875; *Corinne Daily Mail,* Aug. 18, 20, 27, 1875.

33. *Salt Lake Tribune,* Aug. 20, 1875.

34. Madsen, *Corinne: The Gentile Capital of Utah,* pp. 286–88; Young to Staines, Aug. 27, 1875, Brigham Young, Letter Books, roll 21.

35. Danilson to CIA, Oct. 4, 1875, Fort Hall Letter Book, p. 309; *Annual Report, 1875,* 547.

36. Madsen, *The Northern Shoshoni,* 97–99.

37. *Corinne Daily Mail,* Aug. 18, 1875.

7. *LAST YEARS AT FORT HALL*

1. Danilson to CIA, Feb. 7, 1876, NA, Letters Received: Idaho Superintendency, roll 344.

2. Danilson to CIA, Apr. 20, 1876, ibid.

3. *Idaho Statesman,* July 22, 1876.

4. Brayman to Secretary of War, June 2, 1877, NA, Letters Received: Idaho Superintendency, roll 346; *Idaho Statesman,* June 26, 1877.

5. Bainbridge to Anderson, July 10, 1877, NA, Fort Hall, p. 110; Bainbridge to Department of the Platte, July 10, 1877, NA, Letters Received: Idaho Superintendency, roll 346.

6. Danilson to Bainbridge, June 21, 1877, NA, Letters Received: Idaho Superintendency, roll 346, p. 7.

7. Nebeker to Cannon, February 22, 1878, NA, Letters Received: Utah Superintendency, roll 906.

8. See Brigham D. Madsen, *The Northern Shoshoni,* pp. 80–86, for a summary of events concerning the Bannock War.

9. Smith to Department of the Platte, Dec. 25, 1877, NA, Letters Received: Idaho Superintendency, roll 348.

10. Danilson to CIA, Sept. 22, 1878, ibid., roll 347.

11. Brigham D. Madsen, *Corinne: The Gentile Capital of Utah,* pp. 169–74, 299–304.

12. Bainbridge to Department of the Platte, December 13, 1878, NA, Letters Received: Idaho Superintendency, roll 351.

13. *Annual Report, 1879,* pp. 158–59.

14. Petition to CIA, Mar. 2, 1881, NA, Letters Received 1881–1907.

15. Stone to CIA, Sept. 13, 1881, ibid.

16. McCammon to CIA, Aug. 16, 1881, ibid.

17. H. Leigh Gittins, *Pocatello Portrait,* p. 22.

18. Ibid.; Fred T. Dubois, *The Making of a State,* p. 31.

19. *Annual Report, 1880,* pp. 105–6; Stone to CIA, Oct. 4, 1881, NA, Special Cases No. 72.

20. Ibid.; Stone to CIA, Nov. 14, 1881, NA, Special Cases, No. 72.

21. Madsen, *The Northern Shoshoni,* pp. 114–16.

22. Oliver, "The Burial of Chief Pocatello," in *Idaho Yesterday and Today,* p. 26; Newell Hart, *The Bear River Massacre,* p. 267; *Idaho Republican,* Apr. 5, 1928; *American Falls Press,* Oct. 6, 1927.

23. *Salt Lake Tribune,* Oct. 5, 1922.

8. EPILOGUE

1. Union Pacific Railroad, *The Direct Route to Colorado, Idaho, Utah, Montana, Nevada, and California.* See also *Corinne Daily Mail,* Feb. 16, 1875; Danilson to Floyd-Jones, Jan. 12, 1870, Fort Hall Letter Book, p. 25; Betty M. Madsen and Brigham D. Madsen, *North to Montana,* pp. 100, 106.

2. Brigham D. Madsen, *The Northern Shoshoni,* pp. 111–14.

3. *Idaho Journal,* July 4, 1982.

4. Madsen, *The Northern Shoshoni,* p. 121.

5. Dr. and Mrs. N. W. Christiansen, *A Trip Through Yellowstone Park: Interesting Events Portrayed in Music.*

Bibliography

Alder, Douglas D., ed. *Cache Valley: Essays on Her Past and People.* Logan, Utah, 1976.

Alta California, San Francisco, 1863–64.

American Falls Press, Idaho, Mar. 4, 1915.

Barta, Edward J. "Battle Creek: The Battle of Bear River." M.A. thesis, Idaho State University, Pocatello, 1962.

Beal, Merril D. *A History of Southeastern Idaho.* Caldwell, Idaho, 1942.

———. *Intermountain Railroads: Standard and Narrow Gauge.* Caldwell, Idaho, 1962.

Brown, Ralph O. "The Life and Missionary Labors of George Washington Hill." M.S. thesis, Brigham Young University, Provo, Utah, 1956.

Bywater, James. Reminiscences, folder 923, no. 7. Church of Jesus Christ of Latter-day Saints, Historian's Office, Salt Lake City.

Campbell, Eugene E. "Governmental Beginnings." In *Utah's History,* Richard E. Poll, gen. ed., chap. 9. Provo, Utah, 1978.

Christiansen, Dr. and Mrs. N. W. *A Trip Through Yellowstone Park: Interesting Events Portrayed in Music.* New York, 1953.

Coates, Laurence G. "A History of Indian Education by the Mormons, 1830–1900." Ph.D. diss., Ball State University, Muncie, Ind., 1969.

Corinne Daily Mail, Utah, 1874–75.

Corinne Journal, Utah, 1871.

Corinne Reporter, Utah, 1870–73.

Cramer, Howard Ross. *California-Oregon Trail: Fort Hall to Goose Creek, Idaho.* Burley, Idaho, 1973.

Davis, William Stearns. *A History of France.* Boston, 1919.

Deseret News, Salt Lake City, 1855–84.

Dibble, Charles E. "The Mormon Mission to the Shoshoni Indians." *Western Humanities Review* 1 (1947): 279–93.

Dubois, Fred T. *The Making of a State.* Rexburg, Idaho, 1971.

Evans, John Henry. *Charles Coulson Rich: Pioneer Builder of the West.* New York, 1936.

Fleming, L. A., and A. R. Standing. "The Road to 'Fortune': The Salt Lake Cutoff." *Utah Historical Quarterly* 33 (Summer 1965)3: 250–61.

Fort Hall Letter Book, 1870–75, Fort Hall Indian Reservation, Fort Hall, Idaho.

Fourth Annual Report of the Board of Indian Commissioners to the President of the United States. Washington, D.C., 1872.

Gittins, H. Leigh. *Pocatello Portrait: The Early Years, 1878 to 1928,* Pocatello, Idaho, 1983.

Hart, Newell. *The Bear River Massacre.* Preston, Idaho, 1982.

———. "Rescue of a Frontier Boy." *Utah Historical Quarterly* 33 (Winter 1965)1: 51–54.

———, ed. *The Trail Blazer.* Preston, Idaho, 1976.

Hill, George W. Collection. Church of Jesus Christ of Latter-day Saints, Historian's Office, Salt Lake City.

Howard, Minnie F. "Pocatello's Mother." *Idaho Yesterday and Today,* pp. 22–25. Pocatello, Idaho, 1934.

Hultkrantz, Ake. "The Shoshones in the Rocky Mountain Areas." In *Shoshone Indians,* pp. 173–214. New York, 1974.

Hunter, Milton R. *Brigham Young, The Colonizer.* Salt Lake City, 1973.

Huntington, Dimick B. Journal, 1857–58–59. Church of Jesus Christ of Latter-day Saints, Historian's Office, Salt Lake City.

Idaho Journal, Pocatello, July 4, 1982.

Idaho Republican, Blackfoot, Idaho, Apr. 5, 1928.

Idaho Statesman, Boise, 1874–77.

Idaho Yesterday and Today. Official Souvenir Book, Old Fort Hall Centennial, 1834–1934. Pocatello, Idaho.

Kappler, Charles J. *Indian Affairs: Laws and Treaties,* vol. 2. Washington, D.C., 1904.

———. *Statutes at Large,* vol. 16. Washington, D.C., 1870.

King, Jeffery. " 'Do Not Execute Chief Pocatello' ": President Lincoln Acts to Save the Shoshoni Chief." *Utah Historical Quarterly* 53 (Summer 1985)3: 237–47.

Lewis, Jeannette. "The Story of Widzhebu (A Cunning Eye)." Fort Hall, Idaho, December 18, 1940.

Liljeblad, Sven. "Indian Peoples in Idaho." Mimeo. Pocatello, Idaho, 1957.

———. Interview by Merle Wells, Reno, Nev., June 29, 1984.

———. "Shoshoni and Northern Paiute Indians in Idaho," *Idaho Historical Society,* Reference Series, No. 484, Nov. 1970.

Macaulay, Thomas Babington. *Miscellaneous,* vol. 3. Boston, 1900.

Madsen, Betty M., and Brigham D. Madsen. *North to Montana: Jehus, Bullwhackers and Muleskinners on the Montana Trail.* Salt Lake City, 1980.

Madsen, Brigham D. *Corinne: The Gentile Capital of Utah.* Salt Lake City, 1980.

———. *The Bannock of Idaho.* Caldwell, Idaho, 1958.

———. *Gold Rush Sojourners in Great Salt Lake City.* Salt Lake City, 1983.

———. *The Lemhi: Sacajawea's People.* Caldwell, Idaho, 1979.

———. *The Northern Shoshoni.* Caldwell, Idaho, 1980.

———. "The Northwestern Shoshoni in Cache Valley." In *Cache Valley: Essays on Her Past and People,* edited by Douglas D. Alder, pp. 28–44. Logan, Utah, 1976.

———. *The Shoshoni Frontier and the Bear River Massacre.* Salt Lake City, 1985.

Martineau, James H. "The Military History of Cache County." *Tullidge's Quarterly Magazine* 2 (April 1882)1: 122–31.

"Massacre Rocks." Idaho State Historical Society, Reference Series No. 234. Revised 1985.

Mathis, Don Richard. "Camp Floyd in Retrospect." M.A. thesis, Brigham Young University, 1959.

Moore, David. Journal and Life History. Brigham Young University Library, Provo, Utah.

National Archives, Records of the Bureau of Indian Affairs. Field Papers, Idaho Superintendency.

————. Fort Hall. RG 393.

————. Letters Received 1881–1907. RG 75.

————. Letters Received by the Adjutant General's Office, 1861–70. Microfilm M619, roll 267.

————. Letters Received, Idaho, 1865–89. Indian Claims Commission, *Shoshone Indians, et al. v. United States,* Petitioners Exhibit no. 255.

————. Letters Received, 1824–1881, M234: Idaho Superintendency, 1849–80. RG 75, rolls 337–53.

————. Letters Received, 1824–1881, M234: Utah Superintendency, 1849–1880. RG 75, rolls 897–906.

————. Letters Received, Wyoming.

————. Letters Sent, roll 75.

————. Miscellaneous Sources, 1863 and 1866–69, Idaho Superintendency. Microfilm 832, roll 2.

————. Special Cases, No. 72.

————. Territorial Papers, Idaho: 1864–90. M191, roll 3.

————. Utah Superintendency Files (field records), Misc. 1862–63–64, unprinted record.

National Cyclopaedia of American Biography. New York, 1898.

Oliver, Walter Taylor. "The Burial of Chief Pocatello." *Idaho Yesterday and Today,* p. 26. Pocatello, Idaho.

Orton, Richard H., comp. *Records of California Men in the War of the Rebellion, 1861 to 1867.* Sacramento, 1890.

Parry, Mae T. "Massacre at Boa Ogoi." In *The Trail Blazer,* edited by Newell Hart, pp. 128–37. Preston, Idaho, 1976.

Pedersen, Lyman Clarence, Jr. "History of Fort Douglas, Utah." Ph.D. diss., Brigham Young University, Provo, Utah, 1967.

Pocatello, LaSalle. Interview by Mercelline Boyer. Fort Hall Reservation, Fort Hall, Idaho, Jan. 16, 1980.

Poll, Richard D., gen. ed. *Utah's History.* Provo, Utah, 1978.

Portland Oregonian, May 1, 1852.

Rogers, Fred B. *Soldiers of the Overland.* San Francisco, 1938.

Sacramento Union, 1862–64.

Salt Lake City Herald, July 21, Aug. 17, 1875.

Salt Lake Tribune, Aug. 20, 1875.

San Francisco Bulletin, 1862–64.

Sawyer, Lorenzo. *Way Sketches,* annotated by Edward Eberstadt. New York, 1926.

Stapilus, Randy, and O. K. Johnson. "Fort Hall—A State of Transition, 1868–1879." *Idaho State Journal.* Pocatello, Idaho, September 4, 1979.

Steward, Julian. *Basin-Plateau Aboriginal Sociopolitical Groups.* Smithsonian Institution, Bureau of American Ethnology, Bulletin 120. Washington, D.C., 1938. Reprint, Salt Lake City, 1985.

Simmonds, A. J. "The First Settlements, 1855–1860." Unpublished ms. Logan, Utah State University Library.

Union Pacific Railroad. *The Direct Route to Colorado, Idaho, Utah, Montana, Nevada, and California.* Chicago, 1868.

Unruh, John D., Jr. *The Plains Across.* Urbana, Illinois, 1979.

U.S. Congress. House. *Bannock and Other Indians in Southern Idaho.* 43rd Cong., 1st sess., Ex. Doc. 129, serial no. 1608, 1875.

―――. *Report of the Secretary of the Interior.* 37th Cong., 3rd sess., Ex. Doc. 1, serial no. 1157, 1862.

―――. *Report of the Secretary of the Interior.* 38th Cong., 1st sess., Ex. Doc. 1, serial no. 1182, 1863.

―――. *Statement of Major J. W. Powell.* 43rd Cong., 1st sess., Misc. Doc. 86, serial no. 1618, 1874.

―――. *The War of the Rebellion.* 55th Cong., 1st sess., no. 59, serial I, vol. L, pts. 1 and 2, serial nos. 3583 and 3584.

U.S. Congress. Senate. *Message of the President of the United States.* Ex. Doc. 42, 36th Cong., 1st sess., serial no. 1033, 1859.

U.S. Department of the Interior. *Annual Reports of the Commissioner of Indian Affairs.* In *Annual Report of the Secretary of the Interior.* Washington, D.C., 1849–64.

Utah Reporter, Corinne, 1869–71.

Utah Territorial Papers. Utah State Archives, Salt Lake City.

Utah State Militia Correspondence, 1849–63. Utah State Archives, Salt Lake City.

Weir, Robert M. *Colonial South Carolina: A History.* New York, 1983.

Wells, Merle W. Interview. Boise, Idaho, Dec. 20, 1983.

―――. Letter. Boise, Idaho, Feb. 28, 1985.

Wilson, Elijah Nicholas. *Among the Shoshones.* Salt Lake City, 1910.

Young, Brigham. Indian Affairs, Correspondence, 1851–53, folder 16. Church of Jesus Christ of Latter-day Saints, Historian's Office, Salt Lake City.

―――. Indian Affairs, Miscellaneous Licenses, Permits, etc., 1854–1856, folder 30. Church of Jesus Christ of Latter-day Saints, Historian's Office, Salt Lake City.

―――. Indian Affairs, Misc. Papers, 1866–1873, folder 60. Church of Jesus Christ of Latter-day Saints, Historian's Office, Salt Lake City.

―――. Journal History. Church of Jesus Christ of Latter-day Saints, Historian's Office, Salt Lake City.

―――. Letter Books, reel 21. Church of Jesus Christ of Latter-day Saints, Historian's Office, Salt Lake City.

―――. Manuscript History. Church of Jesus Christ of Latter-day Saints, Historian's Office, Salt Lake City.

―――. Papers, 1801–77. Church of Jesus Christ of Latter-day Saints, Historian's Office, Salt Lake City.

―――. Papers, President's Office, Miscellaneous Papers. Church of Jesus Christ of Latter-day Saints, Historian's Office, Salt Lake City.

Index